A History of Charlbury

A painting (c. 1805) of the view down Church Street. On the left is the medieval half-timbered jettied market house, later the Golden Ball and then an ironmonger's, demolished in 1890. The roof over the stocks lasted from about 1771 until it was pulled down in 1871.

A History of Charlbury

Lois Hey

With
A Geological View of the History of Charlbury
by Professor Geoffrey Walton

The Wychwood Press

Our books may be ordered from bookshops or (post free) from
The Wychwood Press, Alder House, Market Street, Charlbury,
England OX7 3PH

Please send for our free catalogue

Credit card orders should be phoned or faxed to 01689 870437
or 01608 811969

Photographs for inclusion in this book were lent by Robert Wilkins from his
own collection and that of the late R.T.G. Smith, unless otherwise
acknowledged

**Royalties from the sale of this book will go to the Charlbury Society
to further the development of the Charlbury Museum**

First published in 2001 by
The Wychwood Press, an imprint of Jon Carpenter Publishing
Alder House, Market Street, Charlbury, Oxfordshire OX7 3PH
☎ 01608 811969

ISBN 1 902279 03 4

Printed in England by J. W. Arrowsmith Ltd., Bristol

Contents

Publisher's note

We should all be grateful to Lois Hey, who has bravely overcome ill health and the advance of old age to complete this work, the research for which has taken many years. Her good cheer and determination, amid a haze of cigaratte smoke, has been unfailing.

I am also grateful to Sue Woolley for allowing us to use the painting on the front cover, and to Adrian Lack for scanning it.

As the book was going to press, Professor Walton offered an appendix on the contribution of the local geology to the growth and history of the town, which we are very pleased to include. It is salutary to remember that history is often at the mercy of events entirely beyond human control.

Jon Carpenter

Acknowledgements

I am very grateful to so many people who have helped and encouraged me. Margaret Rogers of Mount Skippett started me off with the church registers. R. T. G. Smith lent me his books about Charlbury, and passed on the results of his painstaking work on *Jackson's Oxford Journal* from 1753 and *The Oxford Times* from 1863, the census returns and the victuallers' recognizances. Owners of old property have been most generous in allowing me to see their title deeds. Jennifer Bartlett helped with research, moral support and her own lifelong knowledge of Charlbury. Gillian Naish has typed my feeble efforts onto floppy disk, and encouraged me when I despaired of finishing the task. Robert Wilkins has provided almost all the illustrations, Frank Dunn has very kindly done the index, and Adam and Liz Gillicker have made the maps.

My sincere thanks to Jon Carpenter for his gentle goading, without which I should have given up long ago.

L.H.

Jesse Clifford, Master of the British School from 1842 to 1884.

From earliest days

In the very beginning, the land where Charlbury now lies so comfortably was under the sea. The Cotswold limestone, Great Oolite, is made of compressed round sea creatures, minutely small. When the Town Quarry was worked by hand, large ammonites were often found by Ernest Rowles between 1938 and 1960. He also discovered mammoth tusks, presumably from the time when woolly mammoths lived in these parts during one of the several ice ages.

At the end of one of the last ice ages, about 10,000 years ago, the ice sheet covering England melted from the south east. While the Severn Estuary was still frozen, the Cotswolds dammed up the melt water into a vast inland sea, its bed being now the Vale of Evesham. The water level rose until it spilled over at Moreton-in-Marsh, and the avalanche of water carved out our Evenlode valley as it rushed to join the Thames. Water-rounded stones litter the fields still, and were used until fairly recently to cobble the streets and pavements of the town.

Large slabs of stone (or hoar stones) had been carried south in the ice sheet, and these sarsens were used by Stone Age man as monuments. There may have been a Stone Age long barrow near the Youth Hostel. The land between Hundley Way and Ditchley Road was called Hoarstone Grounds, and there are three accounts in the *Oxford Times* – in 1867, 1870 and 1877 – of bones being found when the Ditchley Road cottages were being built. Stories are told of hoar stones being dragged down the hill to raise the road level in Banbury Bottom by ten feet in 1820. The land called Crawborough (Crowburrow, Crawbury), stretching west of The Slade from Wychwood House to Rose Cottage, may go back in time to the days when bodies were exposed for the crows to deal with, the resulting bones being shovelled into small chambers in the sides of the barrow.

Another hoar stone, possibly marking a river crossing, was found when

Above: a hoar stone probably marking a crossing point on the Evenlode, found when the sewage works were being enlarged. There was as much below ground as above. R. L. Wilkins photographed his 10-year-old daughter Isabel to show the scale.

Below: a hoar stone at the top of Crawborough in about 1900.

the sewage works were being enlarged in the 1970s, but it was broken up and buried before it could be preserved. The one at the top of Crawborough Road has vanished. Markstone in Workhouse Lane commemorates another one.

Flint arrow heads from the Stone Age can still be picked up in our fields, and a beautiful greenstone axe, imported from Cumberland, was found in the Chadlington gravel workings above Catsham Bridge and can be seen in the Ashmolean Museum.

Over the millennia, stone tools were replaced by bronze, and bronze by iron. No round Bronze Age barrow is known to have existed nearer than Cornbury, but there are several in the vicinity. Iron Age hill forts are all around us; Lyneham, Chastleton, Tadmarton and Ilbury being the nearest. The Jurassic Way, a pre-historic ridgeway along the Cotswolds and Chipping Norton Heights, used as a main road between the Severn and the Wash, runs not very far to the north of us. At Edgehill, north of Tadmarton, a red horse was cut into the turf, a companion to the White Horse at Uffington, but this has been lost. No-one knows when the square enclosure called Knollbury on the Chadlington Downs was made, or for what purpose.

The hill forts were thrown up to protect cattle and other valuables against incessant attacks from neighbouring tribes; they were strengthened and lived in about 50BC when there was a great invasion of Belgae from the Rhine delta. About 15BC the Catuvellauni, a fierce Belgic tribe, fought and vanquished the Dobunni, who had lived on the Cotswolds for centuries. Charlbury must have been in a sort of no-man's-land between the Catuvellauni on the east, the Atrebates on the south, the Dobunni on the west and the Coritani on the north. Grim's Ditch, the linear earthwork running through Charlbury and partially enclosing a large area on both banks of the Evenlode, is thought to date from approximately the first century AD. It was certainly begun before the Romans came, because Akeman Street cuts through it at Woodleys, near Blenheim.

The arrival of the Romans

Julius Caesar came and had a quick look at the southeast corner of England in 55 and 54BC. In 43AD Claudius with about 40,000 troops returned, knowing that he would find corn, gold, tin and, most importantly, slaves, for onward transmission to Rome. Some of the Belgic tribes welcomed the Romans, and by 47AD Ostorius, the Roman Governor, was in control of the whole of the south east of England as far west as the Fosse Way, connecting Exeter with Lincoln. Our local Roman Road, Akeman Street, branches off east from the Fosse Way at Cirencester (Corinium Dobunnorum) and, in a graceful rainbow arch through Alchester, joins up with Watling Street at St Albans (Verulamium) and so to London. It crosses the Windrush at Asthall and the Evenlode near Ashford Mill (downstream from Fawler). Its route across Stonesfield Common and down into Stockey Bottom by Stonesfield ford has recently been cleared of undergrowth, but any surface stones remaining are covered by the detritus of nearly 2000 years.

Roman farmhouses, originally of timber but later sophisticated buildings of stone with underfloor heating and decorated interior plasterwork, sprang up on either side of Akeman Street. The best preserved in our neighbourhood is the one at North Leigh. Fawler is said to have been named by the Anglo-Saxons *faganfloran* after the variegated mosaic floor of the villa in Bury Close, disturbed when the railway line was being built in 1852. It was rediscovered and a plan of it drawn in 1912 by our Vicar, Canon J. D. Payne, and William Warde Fowler, the historian and ornithologist, who had retired from Lincoln College to Kingham. There is a folk tale that the Priory was built over a Roman floor, but this may be a Charlbury rumour which arose when a Roman brooch was found in the churchyard in 1851, in the grave being dug for Richard Coombs of Finstock, killed by a fall of earth in the railway cutting. All trace of the brooch, said to be of gold, has vanished, but its finding is recorded on the tombstone by the church path. Other villae have been recorded at Ditchley, Stonesfield and Oaklands Farm. In 1995 English Heritage confirmed that the square three-ditched enclosure north east of Lee's Rest is the site of a Romano-Celtic temple.

The Roman Empire began to break up after 400 years of colonial rule in England. In 410AD the tribes in Britain were told by the Emperor in Rome to organise their own defence against Saxon pirate raids. By 418AD all the legions had gone, and the British Celts left behind, who had relied absolutely on the professional Roman army and navy for defence and law enforcement, were sitting targets for the continental barbarians.

The Saxon invasion

The break up of the Roman Empire triggered an enormous population movement. The Scots left Northern Ireland for present day lowland Scotland; every single Angle left northern Europe for East Anglia and the Midlands; the Northmen or Normans left Scandinavia for the land left vacant by the Angles, which became known as Normandy; and the men from Saxony crossed the Channel to colonise Wessex, Middlesex, Sussex and Essex.

Some of the British Celts must have decided to stay where they were, but many were driven westwards to Wales, Cornwall, or over the sea to Brittany. The Celtic village of Walcot must have co-existed with the new Saxon settlement of Charlbury, because Walcot means 'the homes of the British Celts' in Anglo-Saxon, and has the same derivation as Wales. Perhaps the Anglo-Saxon warrior buried with his spear by the turn to Walcot was killed in a skirmish with the Walcot men. You can see his bones and his spearhead in Charlbury Museum.

Written history for the centuries between the destruction of Roman civilisation and the return of Christianity to these parts is almost non-existant; oral history told round the fire at night was only written down many years, even centuries later.

Before the invading pagan hordes had been converted, Ireland, Wales and Northumbria were the only Christian lands left in Britain. Gradually the Anglo-Saxon clans merged to form small kingdoms, and once again Charlbury must have been in no-man's-land between the kingdom of Wessex in the south and Mercia to the north. Fierce battles were fought between the two but, as far as I know, none occurred in our parish. In 628 Penda, the overlord of the Mercians, was victorious over

Cynegils, king of Wessex, and granted a large area of the north Cotswolds to his Northumbrian vassal princes. This included the territory of the Hwicce tribe – roughly Gloucestershire, Worcestershire and Herefordshire – now only remembered in the names Wychwood and Whichford.

In 655 the Bishop of Lindisfarne consecrated a Scot from Ireland, Diuma, as the first missionary Bishop to the Middle Angles and Mercians. The Venerable Bede, writing his *Ecclesiastical History* at Jarrow in 731, records Diuma's success in converting many to the Lord before his death in 658 among the Middle Angles, in the region called Infeppingum. No-one now knows where this was, but in an Anglo-Saxon Tract on the burial places of English saints, copied in about 1015 from a much earlier one, mention is made of St. Diuma, whose relics lay at Ceorlincburh near the river Wenrisc. No maps, of course, in those days to show that it wasn't the Windrush but the Bladon, whose name was changed in the seventeenth century to the Evenlode. In his *Anglo-Saxon Oxfordshire* John Blair suggests that St. Diuma might have created a monastery here along Irish lines, with the church on a bluff overlooking the river, the precinct boundary now marked by Church Lane, Dyer's Hill, Market Street and Church Street. Ceorlincburh is translated by Dr Margaret Gelling in her *Place Names of Oxfordshire* as the stronghold of Ceorl (a proper name) and his followers. As stronghold or monastic precinct, Charlbury must have existed since the seventh century, its curvilinear edge still visible today. Human bones are still regularly found in the garden of Queen's Own, but I cannot explain a reference in a lease of 1590 of the former Barclay's Bank and the present Pharmacy on the site then known as Berriall or Bord Holt.

St Birinus was appointed as the first Bishop of Dorchester (Oxon) in 635 by St. Augustine, who had been sent by the Pope to convert the West Saxons, so in a pincer movement from north and south, England gradually became Christian again. But Mercia and Wessex continued to fight. In 666 Wulfhere, King of Mercia, drove the West Saxons south of the Thames. In 715 Ine, King of Wessex, beat the Mercians at Wanborough (Wilts) near Liddington Iron Age camp. By 750 the Mercians had overrun Wessex. In 752 Cuthred of Wessex recovered some territory by beating the Mercians at *Beorg feord*; this, according to Dr Gelling, has been mistakenly identified as Battle Edge near Burford. In 779 Offa of Mercia regained what is now Oxfordshire and Buckinghamshire at the battle of Bensington (Benson, Oxon). Between 825 and 830 Egbert of Wessex defeated both Mercians and Northumbrians, bringing England under one rule.

The Viking invasion

The triumph of Wessex was shortlived. Scandinavian Vikings, finding little organised defence, had begun raiding our coasts about 787. Because of the precipitous nature of their land, Norwegian Vikings were seamen almost before they could walk. Their polygamous society produced a surplus of young men who had to seek their fortunes over the seas. By expert seamanship they found North America 500 years before Columbus, and on the way they colonised the Orkneys and Shetlands, Ireland, Iceland and Greenland. The Isle of Man was their headquarters in the Irish Sea. They conquered Denmark, and their chief was King of Norway and Denmark. The unprotected flat lands of the east coast of England were an open invitation to the Danish Vikings and by 870 they could be found anywhere north of the Thames.

It was the genius of King Alfred the Great that stabilised England. Born in 849 at Wantage – twenty-five miles from Charlbury – he succeeded his brother Aethelred as King of Wessex in 871. To defeat the Danes, he divided all men of military age into two groups. One group became a mobile army ready to join battle wherever they were needed; the other group stayed at home to help with the crops and to act as a home guard. At set intervals the groups swapped over. Alfred built a navy, and square defence forts based on Roman designs at strategic places. In 878 he defeated the Danes at Edington (Somerset) and persuaded the Danish king, Guthrum and his chieftains to be baptised as Christians. By the Treaty of Wedmore (Somerset) Guthrum agreed that the Danes would only occupy land to the east of Roman Watling Street (the present A5), which land became known as the Danelaw. They also demanded large sums of money – Danegeld – in lieu of sending raiding parties across Watling Street to the west.

During more peaceful times, King Alfred translated important Latin Christian books into Anglo-Saxon. Some of them, in his own hand, are in the Bodleian Library. In the Ashmolean Museum is the gold and enamel knop of a pointer or cloak pin with the legend 'Alfred had me made', found in 1693 near Athelney, his headquarters in the Somerset Levels. In the same museum is a smaller one found at Minster Lovell.

After King Alfred's death in 899, his descendants continued the struggle against the Danelaw, until his great-grandson, Edgar, was acknowledged by them as king. But Edgar's son, Aethelred II, really put his foot in it when he gave secret orders for the massacre of all Danes on 2nd December 1001 – St Brice's Day. One of the victims, a hostage for a recently negotiated peace, was Princess Gunnhild, sister of Swein Forkbeard, King of Norway and Denmark. In an explosion of Viking wrath, King Swein Forkbeard vowed vengeance on Aethelred, and proceeded to burn and pillage southern England until he died in 1014.

Reading and Wallingford were burnt to the ground in 1006, and so was Oxford in 1009. No wonder Aethelred was known as Unready, meaning redeless or lacking in wisdom and wise counsel.

Aethelred spent quite a lot of his time in the royal palace of Woodstock. Perhaps he kept the hostage Princess there, and perhaps she is commemorated by the wood called Gunnhildgrove which stood, according to the 1298 Perambulation of Wychwood Forest, between the Charlbury turn on to the A44 and Woodstock.

Aethelred's second wife, Emma – after whom a dyke or ditch at Witney was named – was the daughter of Richard the Fearless, Duke of Normandy. She gave birth to Aethelred's son in 1004 at her house in Islip, but because of King Swein Forkbeard's activities, the boy Edward was sent for safety to his grandparents in Normandy. After his death in 1014, Swein Forkbeard was succeeded as King of Norway and Denmark by his son Cnut or Canute, who carried on with the raping and pillaging of England. When Aethelred died in 1016, Canute certainly raped and pillaged his widow, Emma, who produced two illegitimate sons, Harold Harefoot and Harthacnut. Canute declared himself King of England by right of conquest, and is said to have married Emma in 1017. Canute died in 1035, and the Witan elected Harold Harefoot to succeed him. He was buried in St. Clement Danes in 1040. Harthacnut – not a nice man – who was the Witan's next choice, died suddenly at a wedding in 1042. Then it was the turn of the boy born at Islip in 1004. After a childhood in Normandy, he had been educated by the monks of Ely, arriving at Harthacnut's court in 1041. For dynastic reasons, Edward married Edith, daughter of Earl Godwin of Wessex in 1045, but they had no children. Edward was much more interested in his young male favourites, and in building Westminster Abbey. On his deathbed in 1066, he bequeathed the English throne to his wife's brother, Harold, was canonised in 1161, and is known as St Edward the Confessor.

King Harold Godwinson didn't last long. He had lived a belligerent and tempestuous life, and betrayed most of his allies – Welsh, Northumbrian and Norman – as it suited him. On 25th September 1066 at the Battle of Stamford Bridge (Yorks) he defeated Harold Hardrada of Norway and Tostig of Northumbria, a close friend of Edward the Confessor. Then he rushed south to confront William of Normandy, who had landed at Pevensey. They met at Senlac, renamed Battle, near Hastings, on 14th October 1066, and Harold was killed.

The Norman invasion

William, bastard son of Duke Robert of Normandy, first cousin once removed (on the wrong side of the blanket) to Edward the Confessor, was crowned in Westminster Abbey on Christmas Day 1066. He and his troops raped and pillaged as the Danes had done, and few English managed to hold on to their land and property. The Normans brought with them their ponderous feudal system, and imposed this throughout England. Taxes, in labour, in service or in kind, were levied at every level of the hierarchy, and order was kept by military garrisons in motte and bailey castles. Robert D'Oilly built Oxford Castle and another at Ascot-under-Wychwood, and other Norman barons built castles at Chipping Norton, Swerford, Deddington, Somerton, Ardley and Middleton Stoney in our neighbourhood. Broughton Castle has survived complete.

The word forest has changed its meaning since Norman times. To indulge his passion for hunting, William designated vast tracts of land as Royal Forests over which no-one but the king or specially licensed nobles had the right to hunt. These lands were administered by officials who rigidly enforced cruel Forest Laws. A local peasant caught trespassing was liable to have his hands cut off and his eyes put out. Charlbury was sometimes within the metes and bounds of Wychwood Forest and sometimes without. But it is difficult to hunt on horseback through closely packed trees. Forest in those days meant parcels of woodland interspersed with open country and boggy waste, ruled by special laws.

In his book *Cornbury and the Forest of Wychwood*, Vernon Watney suggested that the royal manor of Charlbury with Finstock and Fawler was given as part of the endowment of the Saxon Bishopric of Dorchester (Oxon) founded by St Birinus in 635. Remigius, a militant Norman divine who had provided a ship and twenty knights for William's invasion in 1066, was appointed Bishop of Dorchester in 1067, when the Saxon bishop conveniently died. He later decided to remove the See to Lincoln as soon as a new cathedral had been built but he died in 1092, a year before the building was consecrated. Charlbury was not named in the vast schedule of property and owners which King William ordered his officials to draw up for taxation purposes in 1086 – later known as *Domesday Book*. The *Victoria County History* firmly states that Charlbury must have been included anonymously with Bishop Remigius's Banbury property because Charlbury with Fawler and Finstock was a detached part of Banbury Hundred. (Hundreds are thought to have been Anglo-Saxon administrative areas created in the tenth century.) But I think it is possible that the 450-year-old connection with Dorchester may have outweighed the more recent connection with Banbury in the minds of the local scribes. In the Bishop of Lincoln's schedule is the item 'of the land of Dorchester, English free men hold 3½ hides...' Bearing in mind that the information was given to the scribes in Anglo-Saxon, Norman French, or even Celtic; that chorl or churl meant a free peasant in the Norman hierarchy, and that the final version was made in Latin, Charlbury could have become *Angli libri*. Certainly through the ages it has been the proud boast of the inhabitants that they live in 'the town of Free Men'. In the 1978 Phillimore translation of Oxfordshire Domesday, the entry which may relate to Charlbury reads:

> Of the land of Dorchester, English free men hold 3½ hides; Conan 8 hides less 1 virgate; Walkhere 6½ hides; Isward 5½; Jacob 2 hides; Reginald and Vitalis 5 hides. Land for 20 ploughs in total. In lordship 10 ploughs. 26 villagers with 5 smallholders and 3 slaves have 17 ploughs. Between them they have 50 acres of meadow. Total value before 1066 £16; when acquired £13; now £27.

Two of the men mentioned – Reginald (the archer) and Isward or Siward (the hunter) – also held land in Chadlington, and the family of Issard/Izzard lived in this neighbourhood for generations.

I wonder if anyone else agrees with me about this.

The Manor of Charlbury and Eynsham Abbey

Bishop Remigius, as well as his innumerable other properties, held Eynsham Abbey of the King. Founded in 1005 by the Saxon Aethelmar the Ealdorman, with Aelfric the Grammarian as its first Abbot, it was deserted when the monks fled from the Normans in 1066. By 1086 the Bishop had installed Columbanus as Abbot, but then had second thoughts about the location of this Bendictine Abbey. In 1053 Earl Leofric and his wife, Lady Godiva, had richly endowed a Saxon abbey at Stow, a few miles north west of Lincoln. Remigius decided that it would be easier to keep an eye on the monks if the ones from Eynsham moved to Stow, and in 1091 Columbanus and his companions transferred themselves. But Remigius died in 1092, and his successor, Robert Bloet, immediately reversed this arrangement. The monks were ordered to return to Eynsham in spite of the dilapidation of the buildings, and the new Bishop bagged the rich properties belonging to Stow. William II, now King, alarmed at the growing wealth of the Bishop of Lincoln, ordered Robert Bloet to hand over to destitute Eynsham Abbey property equal in value to the Notts and Lincs manors which had belonged to Stow Abbey. So the Bishop reluctantly handed over the manors of Histon (Cambs), South Stoke (Oxon) and the rich manor of Charlbury. The Abbot and Convent of Eynsham were the Lords of the Manor of Charlbury for almost 450 years.

The Rev. H. E. Salter published his transcription of Eynsham Abbey's collection of charters in 1907, and, if your Latin is good enough, this is a mine of information about Charlbury in the Middle Ages.

The minster or mother church of St. Mary the Virgin was in charge of dependent chapelries at Chadlington, Shorthampton and, for a shortish time until 1190, Pudlicote. (Were the stones from this demolished building used to build the Pudlicote Aisle in Charlbury Church? Is this why it is known as the Pudlicote Aisle?) Chadlington, the eponymous centre of its own hundred, fought a long and expensive legal battle to keep out of the clutches of Eynsham Abbey. In the end the Abbey won, but were accused of forging a charter of endowment.

The Abbey's Bailiff occupied the Court House (erroneously renamed the Priory in the 1890s), where the Manorial Courts were held, and supervised the collection of the tythes or tenths of everything grown or produced by the Abbey's tenants. These were gathered in the Tythe Barn which stood, according to Jesse Clifford, until 1860 on the Priory's top lawn. The Abbot had the power of life or death over miscreants caught red-handed within the manor bounds, and the gallows stood on the Fawler Road – the King's Highway – where the electricity sub-station now is.

In 1256 King Henry III granted the Abbot and Convent of Eynsham the privilege of holding a weekly market on Mondays and a four-day fair in August in their Manor of Charlbury. The fair, from 14th to 17th August, was to celebrate the Assumption of the Virgin Mary, to whom the church is dedicated. The market tolls and stall rents would, of course, go into the Abbey's coffers. The Market Place at the top of Church Street was 'Y' shaped in those days, and probably the medieval half-timbered jettied building, shown in the rather crude painting of about 1805, was the market house in the middle of the widest part. There is a suggestion that the Abbey took advantage of Charlbury's new status as a market town to increase its revenues by marking out and selling burgage plots for new houses, on the east side of Sheep Street from the Bull to Fisher's Lane, with rear entrances from Back Lane and the Playing Close, and on the east side of Market Street from the Corner House to the White Hart with rear entrances from Workhouse Lane through to Nineacres Lane.

The Abbey was always in financial trouble. All religious houses were obliged to offer food and lodging to travellers, and these arrived in shoals whenever the king was hunting in the vicinity. Some Abbots got badly in debt to the Jews, some pawned the Abbey's jewels and some borrowed from fellow divines. Constant complaints were made to the Bishop of

Lincoln who, on his Visitations, brought accountants with him to go through the books to see what economies could be made. In 1296 the Charlbury Rector retired, and the Abbot and Convent became the Rector, installing a Vicar and two Curates to act for them. The Bishop insisted that a vicarage house be built in both Charlbury and Chadlington, that 65 acres of glebe land be allocated for the Vicar's support, and he was to have all the small tythes – pigs, goats, chickens, eggs, milk etc. All the great tythes of corn and hay would be collected by Eynsham.

In 1349 two-thirds of the population round here was carried off by bubonic plague – the Black Death – and the Abbot complained that there was no-one left in the hamlet of Cote near the Spelsbury Road to produce any tythes. A survey of all the Abbey's possessions was made in 1363 to reassess the financial situation, and some of the field names listed then are still in use today. In 1419 the Abbot paid 4d for the repair of Charlbury bridge. In all probability this was the one by Fawler Mill, on the route between Eynsham and Charlbury.

On 22 February 1440, two years before King Henry VI had attained his legal majority, the Archbishop of Canterbury signed a charter authorising the Abbot and Convent of Eynsham to change their market day from Sunday to Monday in Eynsham town, and from Monday to Friday in their town of Charlbury. With various interruptions, Charlbury kept its Friday market until 1955.

In the Eynsham accounts for 1448 is recorded the token rent of three barbed arrows paid to the Lord of the Manor by the people of Charlbury for the use of the Playing Close for their archery practice. (All able-bodied men of military age had to be trained to use the long-bow, and had to be kitted out with a protective leather cap and jerkin.) During most of the 15th century the Wars of the Roses raged, until Henry VII beat Richard III at the Battle of Bosworth in 1485.

Anthony Dunstone alias Kitchen was the last Abbot of Eynsham (1530-1539). John Tregonwell, Thomas Cromwell's agent, reported to his master in 1535: 'At Eynsham I found a raw sort of religious persons and all sorts of offences among them… The Abbot is chaste in his living; looks well to the reparation of the house; but he is negligent in overseeing his

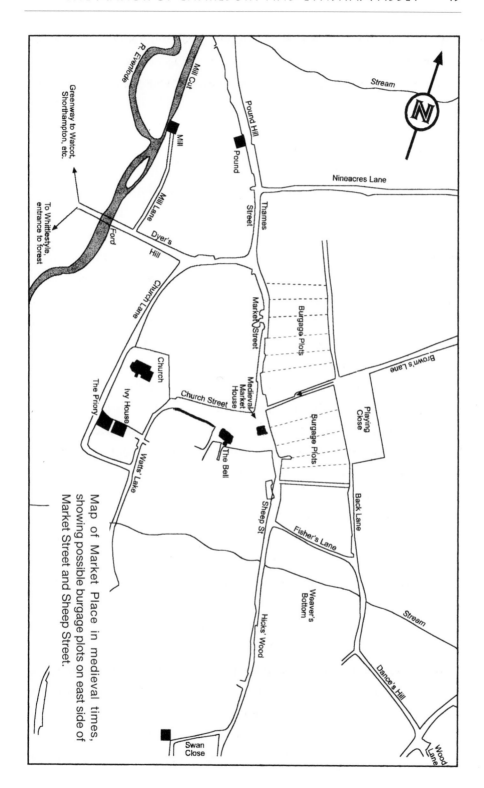

Map of Market Place in medieval times, showing possible burgage plots on east side of Market Street and Sheep Street.

brethren, which he excuses by his daily infirmity.' Despite his delicate health, when Eynsham Abbey was closed in December 1539 the Abbot became Bishop of Llandaff with a generous pension of £133 6s. 8d., and managed to retain the appointment during the reigns of Edward VI, Mary Tudor and Elizabeth I, dying in 1566.

The Reformation

In order to consolidate his family's claim to the throne – there were at least half a dozen others who could bid for it – Henry VIII needed a son and heir. But the Pope refused to allow Henry to divorce Catherine of Aragon, his queen for nearly twenty years. After lengthy and frustrating legal argument, Henry declared himself to be the Supreme Head of the Catholic Church in England, diverted into his own coffers the taxes formerly sent to Rome, divorced Catherine, married Anne Boleyn, and was excommunicated by the Pope. On 10th August 1534 the Abbot of Eynsham and fifteen monks had signed their agreement to Henry's Act of Supremacy, but in 1536 the people in the north of England rose up to defend the old ways. This upsurge of conservative feeling was known as the Pilgrimage of Grace, described in an acclaimed historical novel, *The Man on a Donkey*, by a Charlbury resident, H. F. M. Prescott, published in 1952.

The administration of the country had since the Conquest rested in the hands of ecclesiastics, the only people with wealth and education. Thomas Cromwell, the King's Secretary of State, succeeded in nullifying the power of the churchmen by the dissolution of the monasteries, diverting their accumulated wealth into the king's hands. This enormous social upheaval must have been comparable with the dissolution of the U.S.S.R. in our day. Certainly the ownership of the Manor of Charlbury was in dispute for fifty years.

A few months after Henry VIII died in January 1547, King Edward VI, 'in compliance with his father's will', granted to Robert King, Bishop of the newly-formed Diocese of Oxford (and also Vicar of Charlbury since 1528): The lordship of the Manor and Rectory of Charlbury; the advowson of the vicarage; other lands in Walcot in the tenure of Richard

Eaton; the water mill in Charlbury and the tythes of grain in Charlbury and Cote in the tenure of John Abury; closes of meadow and pasture in the township of Cote and the fields and rents of Cote; lands in Charlbury called 'decayed' lands or ferme lands, and all tythes of the demesne in Charlbury, Walcot and Cornbury Park and all other lands in the tenure of John Abury; Fawler water mill in the tenure of John Hunte; all tythes of grain and hay in Chadlington, Shorthampton and Chilson in the tenure of John Brydges; tythes of grain and hay in Fawler and Finstock in the tenure of William Gough; woods and coppices in the tenure of Roland Graye of Charlbury; the pension of 20s. from the vicarage of Charlbury – all purchased by the King's father from George Owen Esqre.

George Owen of Godstow, Oxford, was physician to Henry VIII, Edward VI and Queen Mary I. His daughter Elizabeth had married John Chamberlayne, son of Sir Leonard Chamberlayne of Shirburn Castle in Oxfordshire, and the Chamberlaynes had prospered from buying and selling former monastic property. But Edward VI's grant to the Diocese of Oxford didn't take into account the grant in 1546 of Charlbury to Sir Edward North by Henry VIII. In 1555, two years after the death of Edward VI, Sir Edward North sold Charlbury to Sir Thomas White, Master of the Merchant Taylors' Company, who endowed his new foundation, St. John the Baptist College, Oxford, with our manor. Queen Elizabeth, who came to the throne in 1558, had been pocketing the Oxford Diocesan revenues since the death of Bishop Robert King in 1557, and didn't appoint a new bishop until 1567. Her choice, Bishop Hugh Curwen died a year later, and the Queen continued to benefit from the revenues of the See for twenty-one years. In 1574 the President of St. John's College, in view of the uncertain times, had the perspicacity to get the Queen to confirm that St. John's did in fact own the Manor of Charlbury with its appurtenances. This was just as well, because on 1 April 1575, Richard Fitzhugh of Beggary, Eaton Socon, Bedfordshire, signed a dubious agreement with Sir William Catesby of Lapworth, Warwickshire (the family connected with the Gunpowder Plot in 1605). Richard Fitzhugh agreed to take possession of the Manor of Walcot with messuages, cottages and lands etc. in Walcot, Charlbury and

Shorthampton, including the rectorial tythes of Charlbury and Cote, provided that no-one else with a better claim came along. If they did, Richard Fitzhugh agreed not to sue William Catesby. But the Fitzhughs lived at Walcot until about 1620.

Obviously forgetting that she had confirmed St. John's College as the owners in 1574, and in the absence of a Bishop of Oxford, the Queen in 1583 granted a 21-year lease of Charlbury Manor including the advowson of the vicarage, tythes and rents of Charlbury, Finstock, Fawler, Cote and other hamlets and Fawler mill 'if the bishopric remains in the Queen's hands for so long', to John Chamberlayne, who had been living in the Court House (the Priory) for several years.

At the end of December 1589 the Queen appointed John Underhill as Bishop of Oxford, on condition that he agreed to the exchange of various properties – including the Manor of Charlbury – between the See and the Crown. At the beginning of January 1590 the Queen granted the Manor and Rectory of Charlbury with the tythes of Charlbury, Chadlington, Finstock and Fawler to Robert Devereux, Earl of Essex, her current favourite, step-son of Robert Dudley, Earl of Leicester, who had died while on a visit to Cornbury in 1588. Two months later the Earl of Essex sold the Manor and Rectory of Charlbury, etc. to Robert Chamberlayne of Shirburn Castle (brother of John) and Philip Scudamore of Burnham, Buckinghamshire, for £800, a sum they had to borrow from Francis Browne, a London moneylender.

As soon as news of this sale reached St. John's College, the President, Dr. Ralph Hutchinson, produced the Queen's confirmation of 1574 as proof of ownership. Hoping to salvage something from this financial disaster, Robert Chamberlayne and Philip Scudamore granted John Chamberlayne a 99-year lease of the Manor on 4 November 1590, before they had to sign an agreement to hand over the Manor to St. John's College on 10 November. They had, in fact, bought it in good faith from the Earl of Essex, but he had rushed off abroad on one of his expeditions and they couldn't contact him. In view of his 99-year lease which just pre-dated the sale agreement, John Chamberlayne covenanted with St. John's College that, in return for a lease of the Manor for three lives (father, son and grandson) he would pay the College various Manorial dues, that he would give 14 days' notice before holding a Manorial Court, that he would put up five college visitors when the courts were held , that he would pay them half the profits of the courts, etc. etc. The covenant and lease was dated 21 November 1590, and very shortly afterwards John Chamberlayne transferred the lease to his friend Sir Henry Lee to whom he had recommended the purchase of the Gibbons' estate at Ditchley, which was going cheap.

In August of the following year, 1591, Robert Chamberlayne and Philip Scudamore seem to have perpetrated a scam on Thomas Gifford, gent, of Middle Claydon, who had married John Chamberlayne's daughter Cicely. Francis Browne, the moneylender, was demanding repayment of the £800 loan and Thomas Gifford was persuaded to pay off the debt. In return, he was promised the Manor of Charlbury, the tythes of corn from Fawler and Finstock, the profits of the Manorial Courts etc., and Wilcote House in North Leigh together with its land in Tappewell, the deserted hamlet in Finstock, which had been included in the Earl of Essex's sale in March 1590 to Robert Chamberlayne and Philip Scudamore.

By the autumn of 1592 the inhabitants of Charlbury, Fawler and Finstock had taken a stand. In all the sales and resales of the Manor, no acknowledgement had been made of the various properties owned in common by the townspeople since 'before the memory of man'. As a peace offering, Thomas Gifford signed an agreement on 18 October 1592 to lease to the inhabitants of Charlbury, Fawler and Finstock for 998 years at a peppercorn rent: the 12th century Church-house (now the Manor House and Sunnyside) where the Manorial Courts were held after John Chamberlayne had taken possession of the old Court House (the Priory); a cottage in Market Street (long since fallen down, now the end of Albright House garden); two acres near the Charlbury/Spelsbury boundary in Church Slade (still owned by the Gifford Trust); and, 'for the only use, profit and commodity of the tenants and inhabitants of Charlbury, and to no other use', the Playing Close and the cottage thereon (now 3 Brown's Lane). The first Trustees named in the lease were George Tennant, dyer, Richard Eyans, gent, Christopher Rawlins, yeoman, William Sheppard, yeoman (all Charlbury), John Petty, gent, Thomas Pridie, yeoman (both Fawler), Giles Camden, yeoman and John Day, yeoman (both Finstock).

John Chamberlayne, who must have been resented as a 'know-all' incomer, had drawn up a list of customary rights and duties of the copy-hold tenants of the Manor containing so many unprecedented exactions that the townsmen rejected it. In 1592 St. John's College and their new lessee of the Manor, Sir Henry Lee, drew up fresh Articles of Custom which were read to the tenants, and they signified their agreement.

Neither Thomas Gifford nor John Chamberlayne seem to have taken any further part in the life of Charlbury, and no member of either family appears in the church registers, which date back to 1559.

The Lees of Ditchley as Lords of the Manor of Charlbury (1590–1776)

In 1583, the year when Charlbury suffered a serious outbreak of plague, John Chamberlayne had recommended to his friend Sir Henry Lee of Quarenden, Buckinghamshire, the estate at Ditchley being offered for sale by Thomas Gibbons at a bargain price. Sir Henry had been appointed Ranger of the Royal Park and Forest of Woodstock by Queen Elizabeth, and needed a house nearer than Quarenden in order to carry out his duties. Before 1592 John Chamberlayne had transferred the lease of the Manor of Charlbury to him. In 1592, Sir Henry, her self-appointed Champion, entertained his goddess, Queen Elizabeth, to a two-day masque at Ditchley, and in 1597 she made him a Knight of the Garter, a signal honour for a commoner in those days.

Soon after he bought the Ditchley property, Sir Henry leased Charlbury Wood from the Crown, and built a house in the middle of it for his mistress, Ann Vavasour. (He liked her to read to him when he was in bed.) The 301 acres of woodland, earlier called Abbot's Wood and later Lee's Rest Wood, was divided into ten coppices, and Charlbury inhabitants had grazing rights in them from time immemorial. Sir Henry Lee KG managed to buy the wood before he died in 1611, and his heir Sir Henry Lee, Bart, and Ann Vavasour – granted a 60-year lease of Lee's Rest in old Sir Henry's will – made every effort to enclose the wood, against the wishes of the Charlbury townsmen. Fences were torn down, cattle were driven in, threats were made and lawsuits brought, but to no avail. The remains of the ditch and bank on which the fence was built can still be seen along Stonesfield Way. The enclosure was to prevent deer from escaping, and thus to provide better sport for King James I, a passionate hunter. The heads of the deer he killed in 1608 and 1610 were mounted above doggerel verses in the hall of the old house at Ditchley and removed to the new house in 1722.

Sir Henry Lee K.G. (1531–1611) from a portrait at Ditchley Park. The dog Bevis saved his master from an assassin one night, and Bevis Farm is named after it. Photograph by courtesy of the Ditchley Foundation.

The heir to Ditchley was one of the first baronets created by King James I, who sold the honour to provide himself with pocket money. The Richard Lee who emigrated to America in the 1650s must have been a close relative of Sir Henry Lee, the first baronet, because his son, another Richard, called his new house in Virginia 'Ditchley' and a nearby plantation 'Lee's Rest'. These Richard Lees were the ancestors of the Confederate General Robert E. Lee.

Sir Francis Henry Lee, the 2nd baronet, married Anne St. John – a formidable lady – and fathered two sons before he died in 1639 aged 22. His widow was left holding two babies, the Ditchley estate, the Lordship of the Manor of Charlbury, and civil war was looming.

The Civil War

Like Oxford, but unlike Banbury, this neighbourhood staunchly supported the King. When the Royalist Lord Danby, founder of the Oxford Botanic Garden and owner of Cornbury, died in 1644 he left Cornbury to his sister Lady Gargrave, but his Roundhead brother, Sir John Danvers – one of those who later signed King Charles I's death warrant – seems to have taken possession. Cornbury became the headquarters of Oliver Cromwell's second-in-command, Henry Ireton, who had married Cromwell's daughter, Bridget, in 1646. Dr. Robert Plot, in his *Natural History of Oxfordshire* published in 1675, said that Cornbury Park became nothing more than a rabbit warren in the civil war. The grass was infected 'by the urine and crotizing of the conies, which being hot and dry, abated the moisture of the deer' and caused them to have very small antlers.

It may have been to strengthen her links with the Royalists that the young widow, Lady Lee, married Henry, Lord Wilmot, a loyal friend of the Prince of Wales, in 1644. The exigencies of war kept them apart for most of his life, but they did produce a son, John in 1647. It was Lord Wilmot who defeated the Roundhead Sir William Waller at Cropredy Bridge in 1644, but I am not sure whether that was just before or just after his marriage to Lady Lee.

After his father was beheaded in January 1649, King Charles II made continuous efforts to win back the throne. He was crowned at Scone in

Scotland in January 1651 after giving in to the Covenanters, and marched south with a raggle-taggle army of quarrelling Scots, to be routed by the Roundheads at Worcester in September 1651. For six weeks he evaded capture, his only companion being Lord Wilmot, hiding in the oak tree at Boscobel and disguising himself as a serving wench on occasion. After several hair-raising escapes, the two found a boat to take them to France, and in 1652, as a reward for his loyalty, Henry Wilmot was created Earl of Rochester. His wife actually managed to visit France in 1654 with her two Lee sons, Sir Henry and Francis, aged 17 and 15, but her Wilmot son, John, aged 7, was attending Burford Grammar School, and may not have made the journey to see his father. There were Cromwellian spies everywhere, and Lady Rochester's visit to France was duly reported to the Protector.

Apparently, Ditchley escaped the destructive attentions of the Parliamentarians through the tact and diplomacy of Lady Rochester. It was certainly a good move on her part to engineer a marriage between her eldest son, Sir Henry Lee, and Anne Danvers, daughter of the regicide Sir John

The First Earl of Litchfield (**above**) and Charlotte Fitzroy (**opposite**), from photographs by Jon Carpenter of paintings at Ditchley Park, courtesy of the Ditchley Foundation.

Danvers of Cornbury. Charlbury had no castle or mansion in Royalist hands within its bounds, but Woodstock Palace was 'one of the ruins that Cromwell knocked about a bit'. We don't know what damage was done in our church. Was there medieval glass in the windows? There is a folk tale of a silver statue of the Virgin Mary being secretly buried near the Spelsbury boundary, but this may hark back to the Reformation.

With Christmas jollity and all other merrymaking stamped out, goods and livestock likely to be commandeered without payment, troops demanding billets free of charge, the use of the prayerbook forbidden, and spies abounding, life in Charlbury must have been fairly fraught. Entries in the Church Registers dried up, but two sudden deaths in the Harris family were recorded – Edmund Harris, murdered in March 1649, and John Harris who died at the church 'style' in January 1660. (Whatever the event, there was usually a Harris in it!)

The Restoration

Lord Rochester died at Sluys in 1658, Sir Henry Lee died aged 22 in 1659, and his wife, the former Anne Danvers, died a few months later after giving birth to their second daughter. So once again Lady Rochester was left holding two babies and supervising the running of the Ditchley estate and the Manor of Charlbury for her younger son Francis Lee (d. 1667), who succeeded in marrying Lady Elizabeth Pope, the heiress daughter of the 2nd Earl of Downe of Wroxton Abbey. Her dowry included the Manors of Enstone, Wilcote and Cogges, which were added to the Ditchley estate. The marriage took place after the restoration of King Charles II to the throne. Their elder son, Edward Henry Lee, the 5th baronet, born in February 1663, married Charlotte Fitzroy, the King's daughter by Barbara Villiers, Duchess of Cleveland, in 1678, after he had been created Earl of Litchfield, Sussex. Not forgetting his responsibilities as Lord of the Manor of Charlbury, he persuaded the King to grant a new charter for a weekly Friday market and for four one-day fairs – the 2nd Friday in May, at Michaelmas (29th September), on St. Thomas's Day (21st December) and on the 2nd Friday in Lent. Not a bad achievement for a boy of fifteen.

The Great Fire of Charlbury

Records of everyday life in Charlbury at this time are very few and far between. It is said that, among other irreplaceable documents, the Churchwardens' accounts were thrown on a bonfire on the vicarage lawn in 1939 by the Vicar's nephew, who had been told to tidy up the study when Canon Payne had to be removed to Eastbourne. However there is a hint that Charlbury suffered a Great Fire in the spring of 1666, a few months before the Great Fire of London in September that year. An entry in the churchwardens' accounts of St. Decuman's, Watchet, Somerset states: 'Collected in ye parish church of Monksilver for loss by fire for ye people of Charlbury in ye county of Oxford the sum of four shillings and ninepence, 13 May 1666'. From North Tawton, Devon: 'May 20 1666. Collected towards Charlbury Church in Oxfordshire the summe of five shillings. Roger Gayer Rector: Alexander Eastabrooke Warden.' And from Wallasey, Cheshire: '1666 Collected Maye the sixte for Charlbury in the county of Oxford the Sum of six shillings one pence. James Ball, Richard Hill, Church Wardens.' The Privy Council could authorise a Church Brief for appeals for aid to be made in all churches at Sunday services if the disaster warranted it. The old Blue Boar inn, now No.1 Park Street, has a date stone 1666 on its gable end. Did the fire consume Park Street (formerly called Watt's Lake) and was the Blue Boar rebuilt afterwards?

The Eyans family

In the Hearth Tax returns of 1665, Richard Eyans was assessed for nine hearths in Charlbury – more than anyone else – but where the house was is yet to be discovered. The Eyans family – spelt variously over the years but with the same pronunciation, Jans, Eyans, Eyrans, Irons and possibly Hirons – were described as gentlemen in most of our remaining archives. The first Richard Eyans to be recorded in the Church Registers married Lucy Harris on 11 June 1573, and it was he who was named as one of the first trustees of the Gifford Trust. His second son, Thomas, left £600 for the poor of Charlbury when he died in 1636. Richard Eyans II had a daughter, Anne, born in 1609, who married James Walker of Shotteswell, Warwickshire, in Charlbury church on 16 February 1629. Unfortunately James Walker died two months before his daughter Anne was baptised on 17 April 1631. It was this Anne Walker who left the lands she had inherited from her father in Shotteswell and Cropredy to Brasenose College as an endowment for a Free Grammar School in Charlbury.

The Earls of Clarendon

Charlbury was on the periphery of two estates which had close ties to the House of Stuart after the Restoration in 1660. Ditchley on the east was the birthplace of John Wilmot, 2nd Earl of Rochester, one of King Charles II's boon companions and the epitome of a Restoration Rake. He died aged 33 as the result of a misspent life – he was said never to have been sober for five years running – in 1680 at High Lodge in Woodstock Park, after a much publicised deathbed repentance, and his wife and young son followed him to the grave in 1681. Although his father had died young, Sir Edward Henry Lee, 5th Bart. and 1st Earl of Litchfield, was more durable. He and his wife Charlotte entertained her father, the King, many times at Ditchley, and produced thirteen sons and five daughters between them. They preferred to live at Ditchley rather than at the Court in Whitehall, and people in Charlbury must have seen them both regularly.

The Clarendon Front, Cornbury Park.

Cornbury Park, the estate on the west, was given by Charles II in 1661 to Edward Hyde, newly created Earl of Clarendon, who had been the King's legal adviser throughout his exile. His new job as Lord Chancellor kept him very busy and, being a bit stuffy and straitlaced, he was appalled to discover that his daughter Anne had been the Duke of York's mistress for four years, and had secretly married the Duke at midnight in the Chancellor's own house in London, just before she gave birth to a son. As so often happened in those days, the infant, christened Charles, only survived for seven months; otherwise the course of English history might have been different. The Duke and Duchess went on to have two more children – Mary and Anne – who both became Queens regnant of England. Both were brought up as staunch protestants, despite their father's conversion to Roman Catholicism. Their maternal grandfather, Edward Hyde, just had time to add the Clarendon front to the south side of Cornbury House before falling out of favour at Court in 1667 and having to flee again to France to avoid impeachment. The poor old man died at Rouen in 1674, in poverty and racked with gout, but his body was brought back to England and buried in Westminster Abbey.

Henry Hyde, 2nd Earl of Clarendon, and his brother Laurence, brothers-in-law to the Duke of York, were both created Privy Councillors by Charles II, and Laurence – a financial expert – was made Earl of

Rochester the moment the Wilmot Rochesters had died out in 1681. Despite the efforts of the Commons to get a bill through Parliament excluding Roman Catholics from the throne, the Duke of York, a keen convert, succeeded his brother Charles in 1685. Anti-catholic paranoia was unrestrained when it became known that James II's second wife, the catholic Mary of Modena, had provided him with an heir. The rumour that the baby had been smuggled into the Queen's bedroom in a warming pan under the noses of the 42 people also present, took some disproving. Charlotte, Countess of Litchfield, who had had to attend the Queen in her capacity as Lady of the Bedchamber, had to sign a formal deposition that no such smuggling had occurred.

The bloodless revolution

The prospect of more Roman Catholic Stuarts on the throne of England was too much for the Establishment to bear, and envoys were sent to Holland to invite William of Orange and his wife Mary, James II's elder daughter, to rule jointly. (They were first cousins.) William landed at Brixham, Devon, on 8 November 1688, and met James II's troops on Salisbury Plain. The first troop leader to change sides was Viscount Cornbury, Lord Clarendon's heir; he was closely followed by John Churchill, later Duke of Marlborough, and soon William of Orange reached London without having to fight. James II fled to France on 25 December 1688 and after a show of reluctance, William and Mary were crowned on 11 April 1689.

The 2nd Earl of Clarendon, said by some to be a 'dumb Protestant', refused to break his oath of allegiance to his brother-in-law in spite of the latter's Roman Catholicism, and retired to Cornbury where he busied himself with local matters. He also wrote encouraging letters to ex-King James in Ireland, and Queen Mary thought it wise to imprison her uncle in the Tower before King William fought James at the Battle of the Boyne in 1690. In 1690 the Earl of Litchfield offered Lee's Rest as a safe haven for four bishops who had refused to swear allegiance to William and Mary, and William Coles, Vicar of Charlbury, was ejected from the living for the same offence. He was immediately appointed Domestic Chaplain to the Earl of Clarendon, and continued to be a respected and popular member of the Charlbury community until his death in 1735. In fact his successors at the vicarage complained to the Bishop of Oxford that he had far more influence over their parishioners than they had. To celebrate the birth of his son in 1683, William Coles had given a silver paten to St. Mary's, and this is the earliest piece of church plate that we still have. No doubt anything earlier would have been melted down to help the King's Cause in the Civil War.

Laurence Hyde, Earl of Rochester since 1681, was more of a 'trimmer' and took the oath of allegiance to William and Mary, who re-admitted him to the Privy Council. Because of his anti-catholicism, James II had dismissed him from his post as Lord High Treasurer in 1687, but granted him a large pension, and Laurence was in a better financial position than his brother Clarendon, who was forced to let Cornbury House. King William called at Cornbury in 1695 on his progress through Oxfordshire. It must have been rather a melancholy visit for him. Queen Mary, grand-daughter of the 1st Earl of Clarendon, had died of smallpox the previous year, aged 32, and the undemonstrative William, as well as most of her people, mourned her very sincerely.

Lord Shrewsbury tried to buy Cornbury for his family seat, but was forestalled by Lord Rochester, who bought it secretly in 1700 to prevent his brother Clarendon from being declared bankrupt. The Shrewsburys repaired and enlarged Heythrop instead.

King William III died on 2 March 1702, and was succeeded on the throne by his wife's sister, Anne, the last of the Stuart monarchs. Anne had been marrried in 1683 to Prince George of Denmark, a fat man unpopular not only with his brother-in-law, William, but also with most of the people. He died, unlamented in 1708. None of his children survived infancy. Queen Anne, not nearly such a strong character as her sister Mary, became a puppet in the hands of Sarah Churchill née Jennings, Duchess of Marlborough from December 1702, Anne's Lady of the Bedchamber since 1683 and Mistress of the Robes and Keeper of the Privy Purse on the Queen's accession. England, as usual, was at war with France; John Churchill, whatever his shortcomings in the way of loyalty to his friends and rulers, was a good military commander, and after winning the Battle of Blenheim in 1704, Parliament conferred on him the Manor of Woodstock and money to build Blenheim Palace. These were the days of embryo party politics. The Queen favoured the high church Tory party, the Marlboroughs increasingly supported the Whigs. In 1704 'Queen Anne's Bounty' was a measure to divert into church hands the tenths or tythes and first-fruits normally demanded by the Crown from parishes. After 1704 the money went to augment the stipends of the poorer clergy, and it is possible that some of it was spent on rebuilding the vicarage house here, though we have no records to prove it. But we do have a book in the parish safe, begun in Queen Anne's reign, recording payments in money and kind to the poor of Charlbury, covering the years 1709 to 1725.

Duchess Sarah became increasingly rude and overbearing to the Queen. Dean Swift, not mincing his words, said of her: 'Three furies reigned in her breast – sordid Avarice, disdainful Pride and ungovernable Rage'. The Whig government fell in 1710 and was replaced by the Tory adminstration led by the Queen's uncle, the Earl of Rochester, who refused to make a further grant of money for Blenheim Palace. The people of Woodstock suffered severely from unpaid wages, and the Duchess went on having increasingly vituperative rows with everyone. By December 1711 the Duke and Duchess of Marlborough had been relieved of all their posts, and went to live on the continent, not returning to England until after Queen Anne died.

There was an extraordinary black sheep in the Hyde family at this time. In 1701, King William had been persuaded to appoint Edward, Viscount Cornbury, heir of Henry, 2nd Earl of Clarendon and cousin of Princess Anne, as Governor of New York. On her accession in 1702 Queen Anne confirmed him in his post and made him also the Governor of New Jersey. On the Queen's birthday he dressed himself up in copies of her coronation robes and paraded up and down in them to impress the locals. He was so taken by his appearance that he had his portrait painted wearing drag! After countless complaints by the colonists about his general conduct, the Queen recalled him, but before he could sail, he was thrown into prison in New York for embezzling public funds. When news of his father's death in 1709 reached America he had to be released as a peer. He died in London in 1723, deeply in debt and leaving no heir. Lord Macauley wrote that 'his conduct through life was a blot on his name and brought down upon him the scorn of two hemispheres.'

Hanoverian times

Queen Anne died on 1 August 1714, all her children having predeceased her. The only possible protestant heir was a great-grandson of King James I – the Elector of Hanover. This militant, non-English-speaking German, who had formed an intimate friendship with Marlborough in 1704, became King George I of Great Britain, France and Ireland, as well as Elector of Hanover, and very unpopular he was. The Roman Catholic side of the House of Stuart in the person of James Francis Edward (the 'warming pan baby', son of the deposed James II) landed in Scotland in 1715, hoping to be carried to the throne by popular acclaim. But he lacked all charm, and was forced the following year to return to France. For some unexplained reason our local Jacobite sympathisers showered our parish church with gifts of silver in 1716. Henry Hyde, 2nd Earl of Rochester, gave a baptismal font and a flagon to fill it with. Sir Robert Jenkinson, 3rd Bart. of Walcot, gave a massive alms dish. Sarah Canning, also of Walcot, gave a chalice and paten. William Coles, the former Vicar, gave a chalice to go with the paten he had given in 1683. Someone also paid for the bells to be recast by the famous bellfounder, Abram Rudhall of Gloucester. Our Lord of the Manor, the 1st Earl of Litchfield, died in 1716, and it is said that Lee Place was bought as a dower house for the widowed Countess. Was it Lee money that paid for the bells, which would be heard clearly at Lee Place? We shall never know whether all this generosity to St. Mary's was the result of a corporate guilty conscience or thankfulness at not having to get involved in a civil uprising.

Enclosure of the North Field

On 16 November 1715 an agreement was drawn up to enclose one of the three common fields of Charlbury, in order to improve the agricultural output. In medieval times strips of land in various parts of a common field were allotted to the tenants of copyhold properties in the town and the ploughing of individual strips resulted in what can still be seen as ridge and furrow in, for instance, the field visible from the houses in Nineacres Lane. It was the North Field of Charlbury that was the subject of the 1715 agreement, bounded by the River Evenlode, Coldron Brook and Spelsbury Way back to the Evenlode at the Jubilee Bridge. In all, sixty three people agreed to forego their right to common their stock on the neighbours' lands in every other year, and to pay for their own fences. The idea seems to have been the brainchild of Sir Robert Jenkinson of Walcot, Richard Eyans Esq. (who must have been the grandson of Anne Walker's cousin who made the arrangements for the Free Grammar School), Dr. John Brabourne the Vicar and Rev. Henry Allen, Curate and Master of the Grammar School. Six referees were appointed to arbitrate on disputed boundaries, and the Agreement was endorsed in the Court of Chancery. In 1738 the Vicar of Stonesfield complained to the Bishop of Oxford, Bishop Secker, that the people of Charlbury still used Stonesfield Common for their stock even though Charlbury Common was no longer available for the people of Stonesfield. The other two common fields – Middle Field and South Field – seem to have been enclosed without protest when the greater part passed into the ownership of the 2nd Duke of Marlborough after Duchess Sarah's death in 1744. (John Churchill had instructed his executors to purchase as much land as possible with the money he left to his widow for her lifetime.)

Local Jacobites

The return of the House of Stuart was still a romantic dream among the local Jacobites, and a row of Scots pine trees was planted along Forest Hill near the turn to Walcot. The Vicar of Shipton-under-Wychwood wrote later that if the Young Pretender – Prince Charles Edward – had not turned back at Derby in the autumn of 1745, everyone round here would have come out in their true colours to support him on his way to London. The unusually large order for bread which young Robert Spendlove had to deliver to Cornbury was discovered to be for the Young Pretender's West Country supporters who had found a safe house on

Walcot. What is left of the Jenkinson mansion after the demolition in 1762 of most of it by the Duke of Marlborough. There is said to be a secret room in the great chimney stack.

their secret journey home. Five years later John Banbury, a barber and peruke maker whose shop was opposite the Corner House, was called to Cornbury to attend an important guest. By the deference shown by Lord Cornbury, John Banbury was sure that it was the Young Pretender on one of his incognito visits to England. In 1751 Cornbury Park was sold to the 3rd Duke of Marlborough, who renamed it Blandford Park, and in 1759 he bought the Walcot estate from the Jenkinsons, pulling down most of the mansion house in 1762. So Jacobitism died in this part of the world.

New Style Calendar

In 1752 the New Style Calendar was introduced in Britain, to fall into line with the rest of Europe. In 1582 Pope Gregory XIII had laid down a formula for deciding the date of Easter – a moveable feast. At that time England took no notice of what a Pope said. But in 1752 here the 3rd September became the 14th and New Year's Day fell on 1st January 1753 instead of 25th March, Lady Day. (Eleven days on from Lady Day brings us to 6th April, still the beginning of the Income Tax Year.)

One of the first items about Charlbury in *Jackson's Oxford Journal*, which began weekly publication in 1753, concerned the revised dates of our four statute fairs. The Michaelmas Fair on 29th September would now be on 10th October, St. Thomas's Fair on 21st December was moved to 1st January, the Lent Fair would, as before, be on the second Friday in Lent, and, also as before, the May Fair would be on the second Friday in May unless this was 12th May (old May Day), when it would be on the following Friday. The first mention of Charlbury had been an advertisement for a very large Market on Friday 27th July 1753 for all sorts of beasts and merchandise. A very large sheep, 7 feet long and weighing about 40 stones, was to be roasted whole in the Market Place, and there would be a variety of diversions and pastimes. Stall rents were very reasonable, and it would be toll-free for every sort of beast. Twenty five years later the Ram Fair became the Ox Roast.

The weekly Friday Market suffered a decline at the beginning of the 18th century because of the disastrous smallpox epidemics in 1712 and 1718/19. It was probably at that time that the Market Place was encroached on by the cottages now in front of the Bell Hotel up to the top of Church Street. The old Market House, a medieval half-timbered jettied building, demolished in 1890, stood in the centre of the wide Market Place, later becoming 'The Golden Ball' alehouse, then a butcher's shop, an ironmonger's and now an estate agents. The 1761 Thomas Pride map shows a permanent open stall or shambles in front of Albright House, but not the rather crude edifice sheltering the stocks. (According to the watercolour of *circa* 1805 in the Museum, the stocks had five holes – were there one-legged delinquents as well as two-legged here?)

Smallpox continued to be a scourge. In 1766 an apothecary, Edward Lyster (?1725-1804), came to Charlbury with his family to help. He established an isolation clinic at Walborough House in Patch Riding, Finstock, for those he had innoculated, and paid regular visits to nearby market towns. For those suffering from the disease Charlbury had its own Pest House, probably built during the 1718 epidemic, on Pest House Piece (now Nineacres Close). Edward Lyster's treatment proved very successful, and it was announced in *Jackson's Oxford Journal* of 2nd October 1773 that there was no smallpox in Charlbury. The notice was signed by ten of the leading inhabitants, five of them landlords of the main inns, who must have been having rather a thin time. Edward Jenner (1749-1823) who began practising on the other side of the Cotswolds at Berkeley, Glos, is credited with the discovery of vaccination against smallpox, but I believe that Edward Lyster of Charlbury beat him to it.

The President and Scholars of St. John the Baptist College, Oxford, resume the Lordship of the Manor (1776–1857)

When the last male Lee – Robert, 4th and last Earl of Litchfield, – died in 1776, the President and Scholars of St. John's declined to renew the lease of the Manor and took it back into their own hands. James Morrell was appointed Gentleman Steward of the Manor, and records of the Manorial Courts dealing with transfers of copyhold properties become clearer and more numerous. One of his successors was delightfully called Prince Tubb.

Charlbury did quite well with a property in Banbury which had been bought with money left by Thomas Eyans in 1636 for the benefit of the poor of the town. In the 1780s the tenant was a Mr. Fennemore, who was not always prompt with his rent, but the property bordered the new Birmingham to Oxford Canal, and the Canal Company bought it at a handsome profit to the Charlbury Trustees. The full length of the canal was opened on 1st Jan.1790, and the price of coal fell to within reach of all but the poorest.

After several severe storms, the stone spire on Spelsbury Church fell through the nave roof in 1774, and for a few months Spelsbury marriages took place in Charlbury, according to a note in our Marriage Register. Part of Banbury Parish Church also collapsed, and in 1790 the standing parts were blown up with gunpowder. One of the churchwardens was a lawyer called Oliver Aplin, who sold the resulting material, including memorials and pews, pocketing the proceeds. This incensed the parishioners, and he was forced to leave Banbury, taking refuge at Ivy House, Charlbury, where he continued his legal practice.

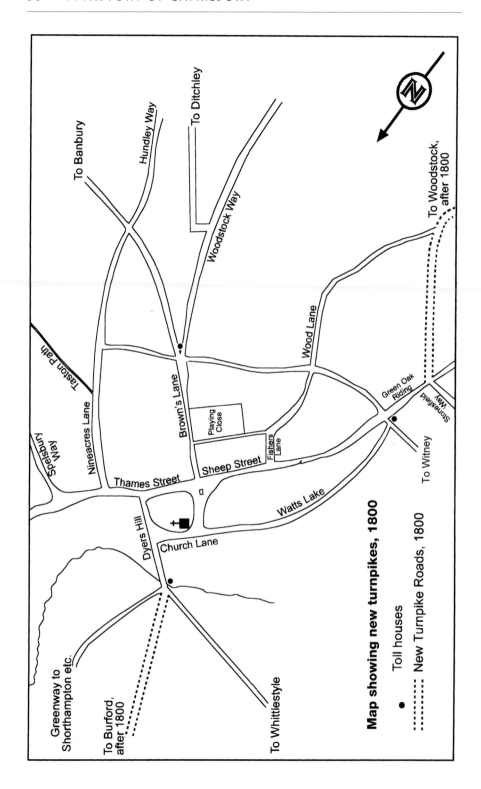

Map showing new turnpikes, 1800

- Toll houses
- New Turnpike Roads, 1800

To Banbury

Hundley Way

To Ditchley

Woodstock Way

To Woodstock, after 1800

Taston path

Wood Lane

Brown's Lane

Green Oak Riding

Spelsbury Way

Nineacres Lane

Playing Close

Fishers Lane

Stonesfield Way

Thames Street

Sheep Street

To Witney

Dyers Hill

Church Lane

Watts Lake

Greenway to Shorthampton etc.

To Burford, after 1800

To Whittlestyle

Lee Place became the home of Benjamin Holloway, Esq., and his wife, Susannah, in 1777, and succeeding Benjamin Holloways took their place as the leading local gentry for over a hundred years.

To finance the American War of Independence and, from 1793, the war with France, Parliament imposed taxes on a great number of things. An Excise Officer was stationed here to collect fees for licences to shoot game, possess guns, clocks, horses, carriages, menservants, maidservants, to use hair powder, and to sell patent medicines, perfumes, hats and gloves, which may have put a damper on our local gloving industry.

Men of military age had to draw lots for armed service, and *Jackson's Oxford Journal* printed several advertisements offering £30 to anyone willing to go as a substitute for a Charlbury man. Wychwood Forest was filled with the sound of saws as oak trees were felled to build ships for the Navy. Perhaps Nelson's HMS Victory had some Forest timber in it. In 1809 the Navy Office was advertising contracts for the conveyance of 555 loads of oak timber from Wychwood to Deptford, where the main dock-yard was.

Turnpike roads

The year 1800 saw the formation of a Turnpike Trust for this neighbourhood. The General Turnpike Act of 1773 empowered local trustees to collect tolls in return for improved roads and their maintenance. Two of these roads came through Charlbury: from Witney through Hailey, Ramsden, Finstock, Charlbury, Enstone and Great Tew to Swerford Heath, where it joined the Turnpike to Banbury, and from the Woodstock to Enstone Turnpike at the Marlborough Arms (formerly the New Inn) along a new route to Charlbury, across Dyer's Hill Bridge, on another new stretch up Forest Hill, skirting the Forest boundary, to the Chipping Norton to Burford Turnpike. The old road to Woodstock went up Dustfield (now Quarry) Lane to the old drover's road or saltway that marks our eastern parish boundary. There were three gatehouses here guarding tall-hung gates (to prevent horsemen from jumping them) and a wicket gate for foot travellers. Baywell Gatehouse (demolished in the 1960s for road widening) commanded both the Witney and Woodstock

Top: Baywell toll house with Wellington Cottage (later Wellington House) in the background. The toll house was demolished in the 1960s for road widening at Fiveways.
Bottom: Brown's Lane toll house (still standing) in about 1910.

Turnpikes. Brown's Lane Gate dealt with travellers to and from Enstone. The gatehouse at Dyer's Hill Bridge was built at river level, but when the bridge was widened and raised 10 feet in 1876 it was disguised by having an upper storey built on. The roads were dis-turnpiked in 1877.

With the improvement of the roads, stage coaches proliferated and Road Enstone became a flourishing staging post with many coaching inns. Letters for Charlbury were dropped off by the mail coaches at Enstone, and were collected from there by members of the Wallden family in a cart drawn by two dogs. Before the Penny Post was inaugurated in 1840, letters were charged by weight and distance, and the recipient had to pay. Sometimes the addressee was allowed to read the message on a postcard and then refuse to accept it, so avoiding payment. The news of Lord Nelson's death at the battle of Trafalgar on 21st October 1805 was disseminated by mail coaches wreathed in black crêpe, and the victory of the Duke of Wellington at Waterloo in June 1815 was celebrated by coaches covered with laurel wreaths.

Jackson's Oxford Journal records many interesting events in Charlbury in the first half of the nineteenth century. In the 1820s an annual Gooseberry Show was held at the White Hart in July, followed by a sumptuous dinner, tickets 2/6d. The heaviest single berry won the prize, and a similar competition is still held in the north of England. A group called the Ethiopian Serenaders (forerunners of the Black and White Minstrels?) gave several concerts. Steeplechases over a four mile course starting and finishing on Banbury Hill were very popular. Bare-knuckle prize fights were illegally held at Whitty Green in the Forest, and local magistrates were taken to task for not stopping them. (As most J.P.s were local Vicars, they would obviously be the last to be told.) Thieves were still transported to Botany Bay, and murderers were hanged as a public spectacle until 1846, when the audience was restricted to half a dozen officials.

Fox hunting became extremely popular. Lord Francis Almeric Spencer who was created Baron Churchill of Wychwood in 1815, rented Cornbury House to the 5th and 6th Dukes of Beaufort for the hunting season. Kennels were built by the lake at Southill, and several houses in Charlbury were regularly advertised to let as hunting boxes. Later the Beauforts rented Heythrop House, but this burnt down in 1831. In 1835 the 6th Duke sold his pack of hounds to a consortium of local landowners for £400 and retired to his seat at Badminton. William Jones, the Quaker weaver who lived at what is now the Pharmacy in Market Street, used to call the Duchess 'Neighbour Buffet' when she went to see him.

In 1834 Boards of Guardians of the Poor were established by Act of Parliament, and parishes were compulsorily amalgamated into 'unions'. Charlbury's own workhouse, built probably in the early 1700s on the upper side of the strip of ground belonging to the The Glover's Arms, now The Oxford House, was closed; 'out' relief provided for the poor and sick in their own homes was abolished, and after a strict means test they were sent to Chipping Norton Union Workhouse where conditions were made as unpleasant as possible to encourage them to find work and become self-supporting. Thank heaven we live in more compassionate times.

Records consulted

A census of the population of Great Britain was taken every ten years from 1801, but the first three dealt only with numbers in each parish and a rough indication of occupations. Not until 1841 were names noted, those who were deaf or blind indicated, and ages were rounded down to the nearest term of five. The 1851 census gave accurate ages and place of birth, marital status and relationship to the head of the house, as well as occupation. Under the hundred year rule, the census of 1891 is the last census available to the public. These returns are invaluable for tracing one's ancestors.

The Charlbury Tythe Award of 1847 is also a very useful document. A map of the parish on which each property is numbered, and the accompanying Schedule giving the name of the owner, occupier, usage, extent in acres, roods and perches, was drawn up to enable the Tythe Commissioners to commute rent in kind into a rental in money. This was still along the lines of Great and Small Tythes, the first due to the Rector and the second to the Vicar. So we have a snapshot of Charlbury as it was in that year.

The railway

On Saturday 7th May 1853 the directors of the Oxford, Worcester and Wolverhampton Railway Co. travelled on the new line to declare it open. Although it was pouring with rain, the entire route was lined with sightseers waving their good wishes. Charlbury Station, rebuilt later to a design by the great engineer Isambard Kingdom Brunel, was decorated with flags, evergreens and flowers. The church bells rang a merry peal, the Charlbury Band played lively airs, and there was much rejoicing.

It was originally intended to build the station near the bottom of Park Street, but strong objections from Benjamin Whippy, Esq., of Lee Place forced its resiting to the bottom of Dyer's Hill. The line was, of course, built by manual labour – there were no earth-moving machines in those days – and of the thousands of navvies employed, four local lads suffered grievously from the speed at which the line was built. Richard Coombes of Finstock was killed by an earth fall in 1851 – his tombstone is on the left of the path from Church Street to the Church porch – and three others from local villages were seriously injured in 1852.

The Forest Fair

Back in 1795 three Wesleyan Methodist families – the Earlys of Witney, the Pains of Fawler Mill and the Boltons of Witney and Manor Farm, Finstock – decided that they would have a quiet family picnic in Wychwood Forest to escape the debauchery of Witney Feast. But within a remarkably short time the event proved a magnet for the entire county, gentry included. On the 19th of September 1807 *Jackson's Oxford Journal* reported the twelfth anniversary meeting and estimated that 10,000 people attended, in good weather with a full moon to illuminate the 'nocturnal orgies', and no accident of any consequence occurred. By then the meeting had been moved to the Wednesday after Witney Feast; soon it spread over the Wednesday and Thursday, and the showmen and circuses moved into Newelme Plain straight from Witney. Jesse Clifford, Master of the British School from 1842 to 1884, gives a graphic eyewitness account of the Fair in its heyday in his *Reminiscences*. It was certainly the most exciting event of the year from Charlbury's point of view. Visitors

WYCHWOOD FOREST FAIR,

September 12th, 1855.

SPECIAL TRAINS TO RUN AS FOLLOWS.

		A.M.	A.M.	A.M.	NOON	P.M.	P.M.	P.M.	P.M.	P.M.	P.M.	P.M.	P.M.
OXFORD	dep	9. 0	10. 0	11. 0	12. 0	1. 0	2. 0	3. 0	4. 0	6.40	7.20	8. 0	8.45
HANDBORO		9.20	10.20	11.20	12.20	1.20	2.20	3.20	4.20	7. 0	7.40	8.20	9. 0
CHARLBURY	arr	9.40	10.40	11.40	12.40	1.40	2.40	3.40	4.40	7.10	7.50	8.30	9.10
CHARLBURY	dep	9.50	11. 0	12. 0	1. 0	2. 0	3. 0	6. 0	6.30	7.15	8. 0	8.45	10. 0
HANDBORO		10.10	11.20	12.20	1.20	2.20	3.20	6.10	6.40	7.25	8.10	8.55	10.10
OXFORD	arr	10.30	11.40	12.40	1.40	2.40	3.40	6.30	7. 5	7.45	8.30	9.15	10.30

The 8.45 p.m. from Charlbury must be prepared to return from Oxford if required.

A Special Train will leave Worcester at 9.0 a.m., stopping at all stations, and arriving at Charlbury about 11 a.m., returning at 7.30 p.m. from Charlbury.

Worcester,
Sept. 8th, 1855.

W. T. ADCOCK,
General Manager.

NOT TO BE ISSUED TO THE PUBLIC.

Special trains were run from Oxford on 12 September 1855 for the Forest Fair.

were accommodated throughout the town, all the innkeepers set up drinking booths in 'streets' on the Plain, and a continual shuttle service of conveyances was run from The Bell. Lord Churchill, Ranger of the Forest, tried several times to put a stop to it, and only succeeded when Wychwood was disafforested – when it ceased to be a royal forest subject to special forest laws – in 1857. The last fair was on 17th September 1856, when special excursion trains to Charlbury were run.

Changes at the Parish Church

The middle years of the 19th century saw several radical changes in Charlbury. Dr Thomas Silver, who had been the Vicar here since 1828, encouraged Finstock and Fawler to become a separate Parish, and Finstock Church was consecrated in 1842. A pupil at Winchester College, he had been expelled for breaking bounds to go to a concert in the town, and remained a forceful character for the rest of his life. After becoming Rawlinson Professor of Anglo-Saxon at Oxford University, he accepted the living of Charlbury, and added the Saxon tower still to be seen at

Queen Anne House, which was then the Vicarage. He enthusiastically supported the Established Church of England, and the coming of the railway, although sadly he died just before it was declared open in May 1853. His successor, William Wellwood Stoddart, seems to have been a rather petulant invalid. He told St John's College that he couldn't possibly live in the vicarage, it was too full of nooks and crannies, and he wanted to pull it down. The Archdeacon of Oxford persuaded him to leave the Queen Anne bit and just to build on an extension. H. L. Secker was the architect, Cowley's of Oxford the builders, and the Stoddart arms are over the front porch. But he died in Italy in 1856 having rarely set foot in his new building, which is not a thing of great beauty.

Before Rev. S. H. Russell was appointed Vicar of Charlbury in 1857, the Rev. George Jennings Davies, a young, keen and eager curate, was given charge of the parish. During the fifteen months he was here he tried zealously to improve the way things were done in this parish. The inside of the church was completely changed. Dr. Silver had already removed the carved oak rood screen between the nave and chancel. He had uprooted a number of headstones from the churchyard, using them to keep back the earth wall of a trench which had been dug outside the east end of the chancel and the Pudlicote Aisle. The trench provided a 'retiring place' for the Sunday scholars when necessary. An outside stair-case west of the south porch gave access to two interior galleries connected by an aerial bridge. The 'blue' gallery across the west end of the nave was for the minstrels with their sackbuts and serpents. The 'oak' over the south nave aisle provided free seats for the (possibly flea-ridden) poor. Pews in the nave, for which pew rents were paid, were all individually designed. Both galleries and pews were ripped out, to be replaced by low pitch pine pews ranged in serried ranks, and all the texts and pictures were scraped off the walls. Four oak-canopied pews in the chancel – for Lee Place, Walcot, Ivy House and the vicarage – were also removed.

As a Parthian shot, George Davies published *A Farewell Letter to the Parishioners of Charlbury* in 1857, mentioning all the things he thought were wrong in Charlbury.

Tower of St Mary the Virgin, showing the new clock faces of 1885, as well as the new flag pole and the resited weather vane erected in 1900.

The new church clock

In 1884 Mr Benfield, the jeweller and watchmaker who looked after the church clock, had a nasty experience. When he was winding it, the weight fell down, only narrowly missing his head. It was decided that the 200-year-old clock wasn't worth repairing, and a new one costing £125 was ordered from Sainsburys of Walthamstow and paid for by public subscription.

The Vicar's father-in-law, Charles Bartholomew, occupying Queen's Own, offered to pay for two extra clock faces in memory of his two dead daughters. The offer was accepted with gratitude, and the clock and new faces were installed in 1885, all four being a couple of feet lower down the tower than the original two.

Capt. Waller of Lee Place gave a new flagpole for the church tower in 1900, and also a new St. George's flag. The weathervane had to be moved to one side to make way for the flagpole, and this provides a date reference for photographs of the church.

The owners of Cornbury Park as Lords of the Manor (since 1857)

In 1857 Lord Churchill of Wychwood exchanged some of his estates in South Oxfordshire for the Manor of Charlbury, then belonging to St John's College, Oxford. The only privilege retained by the College was the advowson, or right to appoint a Vicar. Also in 1857 Wychwood was disafforested. Very soon parcels of woodland were clear-felled, and the land divided into seven Crown farms – Ascott, South Lawn, Leafield, Potters Hill, Fairspear and High Lodge – all with new-built farmhouses and other buildings.

Agricultural work was the main occupation of most Charlbury men. It was very poorly paid, and when the Union branch at Wootton was refused a rise from 11/- to 16/- a week in 1872, 40 families removed to Sheffield to find jobs in the steelworks. Troops from Aldershot had to be drafted in for the harvest. All farming operations were labour-intensive and for haytimes and harvests almost everyone in the community was needed. Some machinery-smashing occurred when reapers and binders first appeared – at Chalford, for instance – and emigration to Australia, New Zealand and Canada increased greatly.

The coming of the railway in 1853 put new life into the Friday market. The stock market every third Friday in the month was supported by all the leading landowners, and a Christmas Fat Stock Show and Dinner inaugurated in 1893 was very successful for many years. Liver fluke in sheep reduced 1,000 head to 300 here in 1876, according to the *Oxford Times*, and rinderpest or cattle plague (foot and mouth disease) was widespread. Years of drought alternated with years of heavy rain in the last quarter of the century – perhaps El Niño was on the prowl – and several farmers round here went bust. In 1886 all the land in Charlbury owned by the Duke of Marlborough was sold off by his trustees, and the Duke had to marry an American heiress, Consuelo Vanderbilt, to keep the Blenheim estate afloat.

Food was home grown. Many labourers depended on their allotments for fruit and vegetables and kept a pig and a few chickens. Butchers killed their own meat, often bought at the local market. When a cow and two horses died in a fire at Oxpens Barn, Hundley Way in 1874, the nimble poor ran up Enstone Road armed with a knife and plate. Roast meat wasn't often affordable for them.

Entertainments and celebrations were also home made. In the Crimean War, from March 1854 to September 1855, one of the Commanders was Lord Raglan, youngest son of the 5th Duke of Beaufort. When not on the battlefield, he lived at Lower Court, Chadlington, and his victory at the Battle of Alma was celebrated by the christening of Alma Cottage behind Hill House in Park Street. The peace celebrations in April 1856 included a display of fireworks made by 'an ingenious young townsman, John Parrott'.

Jubilee and Coronation celebrations seemed to follow a fairly set pattern. Everyone assembled on the Playing Close in the morning, and were led to church by the Charlbury Brass Band. The Vicar preached a suitable sermon, the procession paraded round the town and the poor and elderly sat down to a celebration lunch waited on by kind-hearted ladies. A children's tea was followed by games and races, and in the evening a torchlight procession went up Banbury Hill to a bonfire. And there was always a 'merry peal of bells' several times during the day.

When Lord Churchill died in 1886, Queen Victoria came to Cornbury to condole with her favourite Lady in Waiting. The carriage and pair arrived on an earlier train, were baited and titivated at the White Hart, and went down to meet the Queen's train. The streets were lined with silent townspeople – it was not an occasion for flagwaving.

The Queen's Golden Jubilee in 1887 and the Diamond Jubilee in 1897, together with the gift to the town of pure water from Arthur Albright in 1896, were all commemorated by the drinking fountain on the Playing Close, opened in 1900. A national competition for the design resulted in 66 entries, the winner being A. R. Gough, FRIBA, of Bristol, who charged £14.19s.10d. John Kibble carried out the work, for which he estimated

£128 (the paving and the steps were supplied by B. Ward & Co. of George Street, Westminster for a further £16.19s.0d), but as soon as it was put up it became an Aunt Sally for stone throwers. The glass globe light on the top, made by J. W. Singer & Co. of Frome for £5, was the first to go, but the

Above: The opening of the drinking fountain on the Playing Close by the donor, Harvey du Cros of Cornbury Park, on 25 August 1900.
Below: Another view of the drinking fountain in all its newborn glory

The west front of Cornbury Park showing Harvey du Cros' tower.

stone lions and crowns round the dome soon followed. I believe Dr Juler, who was Chairman of the Parish Council in the 1970s, arranged for the lions and crowns to be put back, but exactly the same thing happened. Those lions that survived were removed and put in the cellars at the Corner House. To celebrate the millennium, they are back around the dome.

When Lord Churchill died in 1886, Cornbury Park was let for 14 years to L. M. Wynne, the aspiring Conservative candidate for North Oxfordshire, a lawyer. In spite of much hospitality dispensed to possible supporters, the Liberal, Sir Bernard Samuelson, a Banbury industrialist, won the seat in 1891. In 1896 Mr Wynne was made spectacularly bank-rupt after gambling on the Stock Exchange, and Cornbury was put up for sale. Harvey du Cros, Chairman of the Dunlop Pneumatic Tyre Co., bought it and spent many thousands on bringing it up to date. He also added a square tower copied from the ones at Osborne House, but this lasted only for about five years before being demolished by the next owner. Harvey du Cros relished being Lord of the Manor. He revived the Manorial Court on Easter Monday when sales of copyhold properties were officially ratified. The Court was held at the White Hart and was followed by a Manorial dinner for all his tenants, with his Steward of the Manor taking the chair. He paid most of the cost of the drinking fountain (£150) and was the official opener at the ceremony on 25 August 1900.

But in 1901 he was forced to sell Cornbury. His partner at Dunlop had fiddled the books and there was a cash flow problem. Luckily Vernon James Watney, with brewery money behind him, bought the estate, and the du Cros family moved to a much smaller property on the Thames near Wallingford. In August 1905 thirty-five Charlbury tradesmen thoroughly enjoyed a river trip from Oxford to the landing stage at Howbery Park where tea on the lawn was provided by Mrs du Cros.

The 1897 vaccination riot

In 1853 the vaccination of children was made compulsory by law. Poor hygiene meant that many died as a result, and by 1896 mounting opposition resulted in the setting up of a Royal Commission of Enquiry into its effects. Before its report was published the law continued to be enforced, and ten Charlbury parents were fined 13/6d for failure to obey. They refused to pay, and on February 6th 1897 a Superintendent of Police and nine constables descended simultaneously on the homes of nine of the parents, marking items to sell to cover the fine and costs. The Town Cryer was sent round to announce that the auction would begin at 12.30, and a large crowd, accompanied by the Charlbury Brass Band, gathered at the

F. T. Horniblow's shop (now News & Things) in Sheep Street about 1897.

bottom of Church Street, outside Dan Kitching's house. The noise was so great that no bids could be heard, and the Chief Constable decided that no sale had been made. The band played *Rule Britannia* almost non-stop and the crowd moved up to The Bull where items belonging to W.H. Baughan, Thomas Lainchbury and F.T. Horniblow were held up. The only bid made was £1 for a Horniblow table, but the bidder was nearly lynched. Before order could be restored an enthusiastic bandsman blew his cornet into a constable's ear and in the resulting scuffle the mouthpiece was broken off and a window was broken. The crowd then moved quietly along Sheep Street where a young man was lying gravely ill, but at Hixet Wood the noise broke out again, and rotten eggs, mud, flour and rice were thrown about. Marked furniture from the homes of Winter and Siford had to be returned, and the crowd and the now perspiring band marched through Fisher's Lane to the Playing Close. At blacksmith Walter Widdows' (Anvil Cottage) the noise was augmented by two of his men beating a sheet of iron, and his double perambulator was not sold. At Edward Widdows' (Elmstead), to the great amusement of the crowd, a bag of flour burst on the head of the auctioneer, who took on a piebald appearance. No sale was made, nor was there a bid for a sewing machine owned by Haynes in Market Street. That was the last on the list and everyone trooped down Dyer's Hill to Sgt. Timms' police station in Church Lane. The auctioneer (E.J. Brooks of Oxford) escaped out of the back door, reached his conveyance and returned to Oxford.

The same evening, effigies of the auctioneer and the cattle dealer who had made the only bid, were burnt on a bonfire on the Playing Close along with a dead calf, signifying the vaccine.

At the Oxford Summer Assizes, 19 men were brought before the Lord Chief Justice accused of riotous assembly and 12 of them were accused of conspiracy to defeat the course of justice. Defence Counsel argued that most of them had only come to listen to the band. They all pleaded guilty to unlawful assembly, and the Judge bound them over to keep the peace. Shortly after, the law on compulsory vaccination was repealed.

Schools, dissenters, gloving, pubs

SCHOOLS

The Free Grammar School

Henry Shadd is the earliest known schoolmaster in Charlbury. Before 1837 the road from The Marlborough Arms up to the Lee Place wall was called Shadd's Hill, so perhaps he lived and taught in the two cottages which were demolished in 1837 to make way for the new Grammar School rooms. Perhaps he became a Quaker after hearing Ann Downer preach here in 1656, but in 1663 he was forbidden to teach because of his religion.

Charlbury's Free Grammar School opened its doors in 1675. Anne Walker, baptised here in April 1631, two months after the death of her father James, wanted to help with the education of the poor children of the town. Her mother was one of the influential and philanthropic Eyans (Irons) family, active here in the 16th and 17th centuries. In her will, proved in 1667, Anne Walker left the lands she had inherited from her father in Shotteswell, Warwickshire, and Cropredy, Oxon, to Brasenose College, Oxford, as an endowment for a free grammar school, provided that the town agreed to refurbish the Town House (formerly the Church House, part of the Thomas Gifford Trust) which had fallen into disrepair.

Richard Eyans, Anne's uncle and executor, began the arrangements, basing the school statutes on those for Witney Grammar School, but he died before the scheme was in operation. His son, another Richard Eyans, Anne's cousin, completed the formalities, but he omitted an original stipulation that the Master should not be in holy orders. The first Master was, by popular demand, Moses Greenwood, who had obviously proved his worth as a schoolmaster here. He was the nephew of Dr. Daniel Greenwood, Principal of Brasenose College until his removal from office

The Old Manor House and Sunnyside on the site of the thirteenth-century Church House. Known in the seventeenth century as the Town House, where Manorial Courts were held: it became the Free Grammar School in 1675. Photographed in the 1930s before the iron railings were removed as part of the 'war effort'.

in 1660 because of his Presbyterian tendencies; this element of dissent probably appealed to the town. However, Moses Greenwood died in 1680, and for most of its life the Master was also a Curate of St. Mary's. Anne Walker's lands settled on Brasenose College were expected to produce £60 a year, of which £40 would be the salary of the Master, £10 would pay the fees at Brasenose for two scholars, preferably from Charlbury, and £10 would recompense the College for their pains in visiting and governing the school.

In about 1810 Finstock and Fawler, joint owners with Charlbury of the Town House under the Gifford Trust, decided that they wanted to cash in their half of the building – now Sunnyside. It was sold to George Malins, a plumber and glazier, who took possession not only of Sunnyside but also of the whole garden, the well, and the range of outbuildings on the North boundary, which he converted into six cottages known as Churchyard Row (now Minster Cottage). He also had the temerity to charge £10 a year for the use by the Master and boys of the pump and privy in the garden.

By this time the remaining half of the Town House – now the Manor House – was very dilapidated, and in 1833 the Rev. Thomas Oakley, Master of the Grammar School and Curate of St. Mary's, resigned his posts and moved to Enstone, where he married into the Marshall family and became Enstone's Vicar. Nobody could be found to take on the school, which had to close for two years. However in 1835 John Hills, a schoolmaster from Swalcliffe, was persuaded to become the Master, and the following year he married Sarah Kinch, daughter of the landlord of The Royal Oak opposite the school. By 1837 Brasenose College was forced to build a new schoolroom at the top of Grammar School Hill, and in 1841 they bought the cottage on the west side of the Old Drapery for the Master to live in, which I don't think he ever did.

In the 1841 Census, John Hills, his wife and four year old son were occupying the premises recently vacated by the Charlbury Academy (now St. Benet's and The Clappers) on the corner of Church Lane and Dyer's Hill. Here were housed private pupils whose fees augmented the pitifully small salary of £40 a year, and who were taught in the new schoolroom alongside the local boys. Unfortunately John Hills died in 1849 at the early age of 44 – according to John Kibble he had a withered right arm, so he can't have been strong. He was succeeded by Henry Rowley, who became a Missionary in Central Africa after his wife died, followed in 1855 by George Morris, the last Master of the Grammar School. Born in Pimlico, London, in 1830, he was an astute businessman, at the time of his death in1913 being the second largest landowner in Charlbury.

Maybe he ought to have been a chemist and druggist, rather than a schoolmaster. His elder son, Henry William George Morris, established the first Pharmacy in Market Street in 1900, and any recorded examination successes won by Grammar School pupils were from the Pharmaceutical Society. In 1864 he bought both parts of the premises on the corner of Church Lane and Dyer's Hill, formerly the Charlbury Academy, and lived there with his pupil boarders until he died. In 1896 the Charity Commission started to take an interest, as the school was in financial difficulties, and George Morris was losing his grip. It was decided that Brasenose College ought not to be in sole control, and ten

Formerly Hunt's Farm, these two houses were used first as Gatfield's School, then the Charlbury Academy, and later for George Morris' private pupils.

new Governors were appointed, Lord Dillon of Ditchley being the Chairman. Nothing would persuade George Morris to resign as Master, and Lord Dillon, not a wealthy man, felt compelled to subsidise the school from his own pocket. In 1902 it was decided by the Governors that the only way to get rid of George Morris was to close the school, which they did.

This caused a great deal of resentment in the town, and a spasmodic campaign was fought over the next nine years to get the school reopened, but no forceful and charismatic figure came forward to lead a co-ordinated movement against a decision taken by outsiders about a 227-year-old local charity. Captain Waller of Lee Place managed to prevent the County Council from taking possession of the Grammar School room without a proper lease, and the Manor House was let to various people; the Charity Commission permitted its sale in 1922 to Burt & Shire, glove makers, for the ridiculous sum of £122 5s 2d. In 1911 the Charlbury Exhibition

Foundation was set up to apply whatever income that accrued from the rent of the 1837 schoolroom and the £40 a year from Brasenose College to grants to Charlbury boys continuing their education outside the town. After many vicissitudes and some maladministration, the Exhibition Foundation is now on an even keel, with a sufficient income to offer worthwhile grants for books and equipment to all young people living in Charlbury who have a place at a university or on a vocational training course.

Gatfield's School

In 1811 John Pain Gatfield and his wife opened a school in the house in Poole's Lane which looks down Fisher's Lane. He was probably the grandson of Henry Gatfield, the last landlord of The Blue Boar Inn in Park Street. Apprenticed as a merchant seaman at the age of 12, he was press-ganged into the Navy and served with Nelson at the Battle of Trafalgar in 1805. A keen follower of John Wesley, he was one of those who encouraged the building of the Methodist Chapel in Fisher's Lane in 1823. The Poole's Lane school was successful enough to move into larger premises on the corner of Church Lane and Dyer's Hill in 1813. Formerly Hunt's Farm, it was put up for sale in two parts – renamed Prospect Villa and Prospect View – by Mary Hunt and her sister Elizabeth Haxby, both parts being bought by J.P. Gatfield. When his father died in 1835, Thomas Pentycross Gatfield, who had helped his parents with the teaching, gave up and moved elsewhere.

In 1836 another Methodist, Richard Thomas Heel, re-opened the school, calling it the Charlbury Academy, but in 1840 he moved it to Mount House, Church Green, Witney.

Prospect Place

On the opposite side of Dyer's Hill this house, now called Dyer's Hill House, was opened in 1840 as a school for girls by the wife of Francis Gregg, a glover, Roman Catholic turned Quaker. Whether Francis Gregg died in 1844 is not certain, but the school closed that year and Mrs. Gregg opened a school for girls at Egypt, the Playing Close, almost immediately, assisted by her sister, Elizabeth Hemming.

THE POPLARS, CHARLBURY.

Called Prospect Place before the railway came, this became known as The Poplars when a row was planted to shut out the view of the station. It was the home of Drs. Croly, father and son, succeeded by Dr. John Chapman. Now Dyers Hill House.

Sycamore House, The Playing Close

In 1829 Edward White Watts, a Quaker schoolmaster, bought this house from William Taylor's trustees. Probably soon afterwards, the roof was raised to convert the attic into a dormitory for schoolboy boarders. At the 1841 Census, John Freeman, also a Quaker, was running the school which contained 12 boarders. When his father, John Freeman Senior, a timber merchant, died in 1828, John Freeman had inherited Egypt, a house on the upper side of The Playing Close, which in 1844 he leased to Elizabeth Gregg and her schoolgirls from Prospect Place, and the schools were run jointly for a time. Caroline Pumphrey quotes some reminiscences of former pupils in her memoirs, especially about the killing of pigs at The Mason's Arms on the opposite corner of the Playing Close. The 1851 Census indicates that the school was in charge of Mrs. Maria Palmer, that it had eight boy boarders, that Jesse Clifford, Master of the British School, was living in the attached two-storey cottage, and that John Freeman, now married, was accommodating pupils and selling stationery at what is now Newington House, Sheep Street. On Census Day 1861, Sycamore House was occupied by a baker from Northleigh, who had recently built a bakehouse at the back, and Newington House was Henry Aldred's shop selling drapery and tailoring.

The British School, The Playing Close

In March 1815 the Charlbury British School Society was established by philanthropic townsmen and women who were disturbed at the lack of education available for the poorer inhabitants. Its patrons were the Duke and Duchess of Beaufort, Robert Spendlove, Esq. was its president, the vice-presidents were George Stratton, Esq. of Great Tew Park and Benjamin Holloway, Esq. of Lee Place, William Albright, Jnr. was its treasurer and James Sessions the secretary. The Society published its first Annual Report in May 1816, which contained much useful information for its subscribers. Although no suitable existing building had been found, the Gifford Trustees had been persuaded to allow a plot at the south-west corner of the Playing Close to be used for a school building. A loan of £200 was raised in small amounts from local subscribers, the first stone was laid on 11 May and the building was almost ready at the beginning of September, but a suitable Governess was not available until 30 October, on which day the school opened. Since that date, 134 boys and girls had been admitted, of which 21 had been nominated by subscribers

From left to right: the original British Schoolroom, built 1815 with permission from the Gifford Trust on the SW corner of the Playing Close; the 1863 infants' block; Oxfordshire County Council's additional classroom built c. 1902. Now all demolished.

from adjacent villages. One girl had been expelled for bad behaviour.

In a few years the original loan had been repaid, and the school was maintained by annual subscriptions from local inhabitants. 1842 saw the appointment of Jesse Clifford, a member of a very long-established Charlbury family, as Master of the British School. It was during his tenure of office that the school was inspected by the poet Matthew Arnold, one of the first school inspectors to be appointed in 1851, who gave it a very good report. Jesse Clifford retired in 1884, by which time most of the original annual subscribers had died off and the school was in financial difficulties. After debate, it was handed over to the Government's Board of Education in 1888, together with the small Infants' School, built in 1863 a few yards from the British School.

In 1891 elementary education became free and compulsory, and in 1902 County Councils were made responsible for it. Judging by accounts in the *Oxford Times*, Charlbury people resented the way in which decisions about their schools were made by outsiders, what with the closure of the Grammar School and the free spending of ratepayers' money on alterations and additions to the Council School. J. E. Barton was appointed the headmaster in 1904, and during his 35 years here visitors from all over the world came to see an excellent example of a small rural school.

In 1927 Spendlove Close was taken over for school gardens, and when W.D. Campbell joined the staff in 1928, the pupils grew all the vegetables for the cookery classes and for the school dinners, the poultry husbandry classes produced all the eggs, and bee-keeping was taught. No doubt the art of pig-keeping was imbibed by the children with their mothers' milk. The gardens were also a delight to the eye and they were used as a public park. In 1957 they became the site for a hideous pre-fab building for the Charlbury Secondary Modern School, closed in 1982, which luckily was demolished in 1998. In 1987 Charlbury Primary School moved to new premises in Crawborough, and the old buildings on the Playing Close were used for further education until they too were demolished in 1998 to make way for a housing estate.

There were lots of short-lived schools in Charlbury in the nineteenth and twentieth centuries, mostly for the education of 'Young Ladies'. In

Above: The school gardens looking north.
Below: The pre-fab secondary modern school built on the site of the gardens.

October 1840 Miss Frances South, niece of the Vicar, Dr. Silver, opened a School for Young Ladies at Wellington House (now Fiveways House), which closed in March 1843. In January 1847 Miss C. Rosier moved her school from Ivy House, Chipping Norton to what became known as Ivy House, Charlbury, but everything was sold up in June 1847. In the 1890s Sarah Cooper, daughter of Richard Cooper, Charlbury's Inspector of Nuisances, kept a girls' school at The Elms, Market Street (now the Old Post House). In about 1899 the Coopers moved to Lauriston House, Sheep Street (now Deanhurst) when the Sessions family left Charlbury.

Merton House, Thames Street (right) was a school for young ladies. Now Grantchester House, the home of Eric and Carla Yorke for many years.

When Mr. Cooper remarried in his old age, his daughter was callously turned out of the house, and had to eke out an existence in a bed-sit in Chipping Norton, playing the piano for the silent films shown at the cinema and giving lessons in her room. From 1894 to 1900 there was a School for Young Ladies at Merton (now Grantchester) House, Thames Street, run by the Misses Page and Castell. As in other buildings here used as schools, the roof may have been raised at this time to provide a dormitory on the top floor.

From 1923 to 1929 a Quaker Preparatory School for Boys was housed in the Friends' Meeting House, Market Street, when it had been closed for worship. Small private kindergartens were organised by mothers who wanted their own 5-11 year olds taught at home – Mrs. Poskitt at The Old Bakery, Thames Street, Mrs. Pearce at Sandford Mount before the 1939-45 War, Mrs. Hughes-Hallett at Ranger's Lodge and the Marchioness of Blandford at Lee Place, after the War. Now there are private playgroups, with the children graduating quite happily to the Primary School.

THE DISSENTERS

The Religious Society of Friends (Quakers)

Ann Downer, the eldest of the children of the Rev. Thomas Downer, Vicar of Charlbury, to be baptised here in 1624, was in London after her father's death in 1642. There she met George Fox (1624-1691), the founder of the Religious Society of Friends, and soon became a convinced Friend. Members of the Society believed that all clergy of whatever denomination were an unnecessary impediment in an individual's communion with God. Ann Downer was the first woman to preach in London, for which she was publicly whipped. She preached in Charlbury and Chadlington in 1656 with much success. In an episcopal return of 1669 it was said that there were about 30 Quakers here who met twice a week in the house of Alexander Harris in Park Street. When George Fox was imprisoned in Launceston Gaol, Ann Downer walked there from London to write his letters, cook for him and see to his laundry. She married Robert Greenwell in 1664 in Newgate Prison while he was under

The Friends' Meeting House, Market Street, before its extension in 1997.

sentence of transportation for seven years to Jamaica, but he died before the sentence could be carried out. Later she married George Whitehead (1636?-1723), who pleaded for religious freedom at the courts of Charles II, James II, William & Mary, George I and George II. Ann died in London in May 1686. She would have known that a Friends' Meeting House had been built here in 1681.

According to Robert Spendlove's widow, his great-grandfather was a Royalist officer in the Civil War. When 'the right but repulsive Roundheads' beat 'the wrong but romantic Royalists', the king's army was disbanded in Oxford. Great-grandfather Spendlove, having forfeited the family's Shropshire estates to the winners, is thought to have settled at Oxford's Castle Mills. His son Edward I, a baker, arrived in Charlbury about 1684 via Stanford-in-the-Vale, where his first son Edward II was baptised, and Coldron Mill, Spelsbury. His second son, William I was baptised here in 1685. I believe they first owned a cottage behind the Friends' Meeting House which had a largish yard, the site still being known as the Old Bakery.

Soon after Edward and his family arrived here, they became Quakers. In 1710 Edward II, a maltster, bought Albright House, which had a malt-house attached. He married Mary French from Hook Norton, and they had three children: Edward, born 1722, died 1743; John, born 1723, died 1731; and Hannah, born 1720, married (1) William Clark, who died of smallpox not long after the wedding, and (2) William Squire of Witney. Neither marriage produced children, and Hannah died in 1780. Edward Spendlove I's second son, William I, born and baptised here in 1685, took over his father's bakery and married Mary Haydon, daughter of an Oddington baker and mealman. They had fourteen children, all but three of whom died in infancy. The eldest survivor, William II, married Sarah Hughes of Witney, but he died of smallpox in about 1746, and their three sons all died young. William I's next surviving child, Mary, also caught smallpox, which so debilitated her that she died unmarried aged 24. But the great survivor was Robert Spendlove. His father, William I, bought the Corner House from John Sutton in 1722, and built a new frontage facing Market Street, incorporating a gazebo on the roof. The locals immediately

The 1725 street frontage of the Corner House with its observatory. It may have been end-on to the road, like The Lawn further along Market Street, and Lee Place before the 1722 west front was added. The Star pub is attached to the left. The photograph is earlier than 1905.

referred to it as Observatory House. Robert Spendlove was born there in 1726 and died there in 1822, aged 96, a very prosperous man.

It was Robert who took an astonishing number of his father's loaves to Cornbury in 1745, where he found Bonnie Prince Charlie's west country supporters hiding after their defeat at Derby. It was Robert who gave Francis Wyatt, hempdresser, a mortgage on 3 Brown's Lane at one penny a year interest, when Wyatt bought the cottage from the Thomas Gifford trustees in 1761. It was Robert who came to the aid of his brother William's widow in 1764 when she and her second husband, Miles Parker Busby (also a baker and mealman), were unable to repay the mortgage on what is now the Oxford House to the executors of Abel Issard. At his death, Robert owned a farm at Chilson, Sheep Street Farm here (now Hone House), Lindsell House, News and Things, land in Crawborough, land in Hundley Way, the fields on which Hazeldean and Wychwood House were later built, as well as Spendlove Close (formerly Joyner's

Close), Markstone and the Corner House. He left a legacy of £100 to the British School on the Playing Close to help with building costs, and everything else to his widow, who survived him by three years. She was Elizabeth Bright before her marriage, one of the three good-looking sisters who were connections of George Fox, the founding member of the Society of Friends. When widowed, their mother came to live at The Willows in Church Lane. Robert and Elizabeth Spendlove had no children, so Elizabeth left Robert's property to her sister Mary Bowly and her four children, and to her sister Rebecca Gibbins, who went to live at News and Things.

The first Albright to arrive in Charlbury was William in 1767, aged 21. His family in Bedfordshire had been regularly persecuted – as were all Quakers – for not paying their Church Tythes. William Squire, Hannah Spendlove's second husband, asked young William Albright to come and help him run the mercer's shop in Market Street. William must have been a good salesman, for William Squire handed the shop over to him in 1771, and, thus encouraged, the new proprietor married Rachel Marshall that same year. They lived over the shop, and had six children. The eldest son, another William (1777-1852) bought William Squire's house in Church Street in 1813 for his father and mother. Within the Albright family it was

The Albright House, Church Street.

The Albright shop in Church Street, after it had been handed over to Thackwell Smith in 1858.

always known as 'the other house' but to everyone else it was the Albright House. William Albright Jnr, who had married Rachel Tanner in 1801, also had six children. He took over the Market Street shop from his father, and in due course decided to move to larger premises in Church Street – now the butcher's. I have not been able to see the title deeds, which are with the Cornbury Estate's solicitors in Reading, so don't know the date of purchase. It was probably about 1825 because that year another storey was added, the front was stuccoed, and a gazebo was removed from the roof.

The Market Street shop was divided into two houses, the better half for William Jnr's sister Hannah, the other bit for John Penson, glover, who had been brought to Charlbury to help William to revive the gloving industry to alleviate the poverty resulting from the Napoleonic War. The Church Street shop prospered, selling groceries and pharmaceuticals as well as drapery. Later, it was also a branch of the Stourbridge and Kidderminster Bank. The shop was handed over to William's younger son, John Marshall Albright (1816-1909) when he married Caroline Westcombe in 1841, the parents moving across the road to 'the other house'. John and Caroline had no children of their own, but brought up

The first Albright House in Market Street (right, with window boxes and a young man standing outside). It may have been a mercer's since the seventeenth century, owned by Richard Harris, and was divided in about 1825. On the opposite side is the derelict Gifford Trust cottage used as a stable by Hannah Albright when she lived in the divided house.

Caroline Westcombe Pumphrey (1845-1925), their niece, whose mother died a year after she was born. Caroline Pumphrey's delightful memoirs – *Charlbury of Our Childhood* – are most entertaining.

John Marshall Albright and his cousin William Tanner bought what is now called Gothic House in 1852. Mary Albright, John's eldest sister, had been living there since her marriage to Dr. William Pollard in 1849, previous owners having been Edward Lyster, the smallpox vaccinator, and Dr. George Horniblow. Mary died in 1876 and William Pollard in 1878, but it is not clear from the title deeds exactly when the house on the east, bought by Mary Pollard and her brother Arthur Albright in 1859, was demolished to make room for the Victorian Gothic extension. The demolished house had been divided into five tenements by George Malins, plumber and glazier, so possibly it was necessary to wait until all the tenements were empty before demolition could begin. Gothic House was used by relations of the Albrights – Sturges, Hollings, Scott Moncriefs et al. – until it was sold to the Revd. Jabez Comfort, Baptist Minister, in 1910.

In 1858 John Albright handed the Church Street shop over to his senior assistant Thackwell Smith, and went to live at Hazeldean, the house he built at the top of Enstone Road. He lived for another fifty years, visiting every Meeting in the British Isles at least once, and was a highly respected senior member of the Society of Friends. His elder brother Arthur Albright (1811-1900) founded the chemical firm of Albright and Wilson in Birmingham, manufacturing safety matches, which is still going strong. Arthur kept in close touch with events in Charlbury, and his many children spent a lot of their holidays at Albright House. In 1879 he bought The Royal Oak Inn, turned out the unsatisfactory Green family who ran it, and converted it into a Coffee House and Temperance Hotel. He built a lecture room – soon enlarged into what became known as the Town Hall – in the

Hazeldean, Enstone Road, built from stone dug from the site. A small tornado whipped the plans from under the builder's nose, and they were later found at Taston.

The windmill on Wigwell Field. Oxpens Barn and Hazeldean can be seen on the skyline.

capacious inn yard. Part of the yard he gave to the YMCA for their Red Triangle Club room, and a mineral water factory run by Bowls the grocers opposite was built on another bit of the yard.

It may have been the mineral water factory's source of water – the well in the inn yard – that prompted another generous gesture from Arthur Albright. For several years the County Medical Officer had been warning about the polluted state of the town wells. Surface water and sewage ran in unmortared stone gullies down the streets, with inevitable seepage into the wells. In 1896 Arthur Albright bought Wigwell field, and water from the several springs was pumped up by a windmill to a reservoir in Ditchley Road. The water descended to the town through new earthenware pipes

Wychwood House. It has been converted into flats and its extensive garden built over.

by gravity, and householders paid the Charlbury Waterworks Co. variable amounts depending on whether they had a bath and/or a water closet. A hundred years later, Thames Water replaced the earthenware with blue plastic pipes, but the pure spring water was replaced by recycled Oxford water in the 1960s, to meet the demands of the greatly expanded town.

William Albright Jnr. (d.1852) had two younger brothers: James (d.1824) whose son Joseph built Wychwood House, opposite Hazeldean, in about 1863. Having left the Society of Friends for the Church of England, he held the post of Churchwarden of St. Mary's almost until his death in 1891; and Nicholas (d.1856) who was a chemist and druggist in Maidenhead who returned to live in Charlbury when he married Rebecca Bowly (d.1840), the inheritor of the Corner House from her aunt, Elizabeth Spendlove. Rebecca Albright left the Corner House to her husband Nicholas for his lifetime, and he married again. His second wife, Lettitia Impey, had run a large girls' school in Worcester, and after her marriage she ruled her husband with a rod of iron. Neither marriage produced children.

Two generations of the Sessions family ran the Charlbury Brewery in Park Street until 1891. Two generations of the Bissell family ran a ham and bacon curing shop in the building which is now the Pharmacy. When

The Bissell family refaced the front of their shop with red bricks from the Fawler brick-
works, and it was known as The Red House in the 1880s and 1890s. Fred Perkins had
the bricks painted at the end of the second world war. The photograph (1884) shows
Edwin Bissell with children.

Arthur Bissell, a descendant, retired as Warden of 43 St. Giles', the
Oxford Quaker Meeting House, and came to live in Charlbury, he was the
instigator of the publication in 1990 of Caroline Pumphrey's memoirs by
the Sessions Book Trust of York, run by another branch of the Sessions
family. Sadly, Arthur died in 1988 and never saw the finished book.

Methodists

John Wesley (1703-1791) was a frequent visitor to Manor Farm,
Finstock, when the Bolton family lived there, and the chapel here in Fisher's
Lane was built on land given by Edward Bolton's widow. It was opened in
1823, and rooms for the Sunday School were soon added at right angles to
the chapel. In 1853 a Primitive Methodist Chapel was built at the other end
of Fisher's Lane to cater for those who disagreed with the Wesleyan
Methodists on the subject of temperance. Later it became a Salvation Army
Citadel, then a laundry, and is now a Roman Catholic Church.

Baptists

It is said that the Baptist Chapel at the top of Dyer's Hill, built in 1853, was needed for the spiritual welfare of the railway navvies, but one queries this, as a lot of them were Irish Catholics. Baptism by total immersion is one of the tenets of this denomination, and the pool within the building has recently been modernised and enlarged. There is an interesting photograph of a public baptism in the Mill Cut at the old bathing place in Water Lane in 1914, which shows the total immersion of Constance Marchant Comfort, daughter of the Rev. Jabez Comfort and his wife Elizabeth (Bessie Marchant, prolific author of girls' school stories) who had bought Gothic House from the Albright family in 1910.

Hyper-Calvinists

This little-known sect appeared fleetingly in Charlbury when Henry Aldred, a local draper, built an unattractive edifice in a mixture of red brick and stone attached to the north side of The Bear beerhouse in Sheep Street in about 1856, which he named Providence Chapel (more recently Charlbury Interiors). By 1873 it had been converted into a cottage, but the stone nameplate for the chapel is in the Museum.

THE GLOVING INDUSTRY

The earliest reference to our local industry is in *Jackson's Oxford Journal* of 28 October 1758. Mary Coleman, whose husband Francis had recently died, advises his customers that she intends to carry on his business of breeches making and gloving, but I don't know where they lived. In 1805 William Dyke handed over The Glovers' Arms (now the Oxford House) to his son Thomas, both of them being glovers. In 1846 Robert Edwards, the then occupier of The Glovers' Arms, appealed against the local magistrates' refusal to grant a spirit licence to his beerhouse. It was thought that on receipt of their wages, his 400 workers might spend the money on gin before they got home. Thoroughly disgusted by the refusal, in May 1848 Robert Edwards sold his stock-in-trade – knives, boards, blocks, furnace, bags of ochre, colouring tubs, etc. etc. – at his workshop in Playing Close Lane (where Tanner's Court now is), together with the furniture and effects in The Glovers' Arms, and moved to Birmingham.

This cleared the way for the expansion of Samuel Pritchett's glove manufactory. He had come to Charlbury from Woodstock in about 1840, with a new wife and gloving skills. He occupied Caigers in Sheep Street, and may have taken over Robert Edwards' workshop and tools in 1848, because in the 1851 Census it was said that he employed 28 grounders, 8 bleachers, 8 colourers, 16 cutters, 8 layers-out, 8 ironers, 8 boys and 822 women sewers who worked for two or more masters. He also had four children and a draper's and grocer's shop. It was customary for one sewer from each neighbouring village to collect and bring in the hand-sewn gloves to the factory, receive the pitifully small payment for each pair, do what shopping each sewer had listed and return with a pile of cut-out skins ready for sewing.

In the 1861 Census, Samuel Pritchett was also employing 12 farm labourers and three boys on his recently acquired farm of 286 acres. But by July 1872 his mortgagees ordered the sale of all his property, which included the tannery, fellmongering pits and newly built workshops in what was known as Weaver's Bottom, the stream valley below Fisher's Lane between the bottom of Dancer's Hill and Hixet Wood bottom. This specially adapted land and buildings didn't sell until 1876, when I believe it was bought by William Bowen, a glove manufacturer from Chipping Norton. He lived at what is now the Old Post House in Market Street from about 1876 to 1890. According to the 1891 Census he was living in the newly built Hawthorn Villa, Messrs. Dyke, Boots and Farmer had a glove factory in Fisher's Lane, George Boots was living in one of the newly built cottages in Mount Pleasant, Frederick Farmer in Knaves Knoll, and George Henry Dyke at 3 Ditchley Road Cottages.

In December 1896 Messrs. Fownes of Worcester opened their new factory in the grounds of Rock Villa, Ditchley Road (later a youth hostel) by throwing a party. The Manager, Adolphus Allen, and his wife lived at Rock Villa, and added greatly to the social life of Charlbury. They were both musical, and – when all entertainments were home-made – no concert was arranged without their songs and accompaniment. In 1926 three pairs of houses in Hundley Way, christened Falcon Villas after the

Rock Villa became a youth hostel after the second world war. It was recently sold for development..

Fownes' logo, were built for their highly esteemed cutters. The factory closed in 1939, at the beginning of the 1939-45 war.

Dyke, Boots & Farmer was taken over by Charlie Hughes in 1927, but there was no room to extend the premises in Fisher's Lane. So in 1936 a new factory in Back (or Poole's) Lane was opened, with room for 60 workers. After the War it became a warehouse selling sports goods and carpets, and has since been demolished to make way for housing.

C.W. Burt, a glover from Worcester, and A.J. Shire, a tanner from Yeovil, went into partnership to manufacture gloves, possibly during the

1914-18 war. They rented, and then bought in 1919 for £620, the homestead and farmyard in Market Street owned in 1800 by George Baskett, yeoman farmer, later by his son William, afterwards by Edward Harris, baker, followed by his widow Charlotte. Burt and Shire demolished an old barn and built a tannery, which became the motor repair workshop of Brice and Price of the Corner Garage in 1931, when the Burt/Shire partnership came to an end. There is a local tale that arsenic from the tannery got into drinking water, which caused the immediate closure of the tannery, but Charles Burt continued to make gloves in conjunction with Messrs. Firkins of Worcester in the building now called Reddingwick House, until it closed in 1967.

Another Worcester glove manufacturer, Dent Allcroft, wishing to take advantage of the skilled labour available around Charlbury, erected a purpose-built factory at Baywell Gate in 1933, extended in 1937. Taken over by the government in 1939, it was handed back to Dent's in 1945, and in 1968 was the last of Charlbury's glove factories to close. The building is now owned by the hydraulic components firm Flupac Ltd.

PUBS PAST AND PRESENT

Over the years, lots of houses in Charlbury were licensed to sell ale. When hops were added to the malted barley mash from the beginning of the 17th century, ale became beer. Six of the main inns also had spirit licences – The Bell, The Rose and Crown, The Bull, The Royal Oak, The White Hart and The Talbot. Pictorial signs were used for inns and shops in medieval times before people could read. Being a market town belonging to Eynsham Abbey the earliest inn signs probably had a religious signifi-cance. The Bell, The Star, and possibly Noah's Ark would come into this category. The Bell was obviously repaired if not partially rebuilt in 1700, according to the date over the front door, but it must have been there soon after the market was authorised in 1256. The Star, between the Corner House and the barber's shop in Market Street, was pulled down in 1913 by the owner, Frank Bowly, who lived in the Corner House. A small twin-gabled house always referred to as Noah's Ark – a very common name for a pub in medieval times – was demolished in 1912 to make way for Alfred

The Star Inn, between the barber's shop and the Corner House. And (**right**) being demolished in 1913.

Warner's motor workshop, now Alan Bristow's office in Market Street. It was next door to and may have been part of No. 1 Downsteps, which has an excellent cellar and a panelled front room.

The White Hart, the badge of King Richard II, could have been so named to commemorate the gift of his hunting lodge at Cornbury to his wife Anne of Bohemia in 1381.

The low twin-gabled house in Market Street was always known as Noah's Ark. It had probably been a medieval inn.

The building on the southern boundary of the churchyard (now 1 Park Street) was once the Blue Boar Inn. The white boar was King Richard III's emblem and he was quite popular in these parts despite later malicious Tudor propaganda. The landlord may have considered it politically correct to give the pig a quick blue rinse after Henry Tudor was the victor at Bosworth in 1485. The same seems to have happened at Chipping Norton too.

The White Hart in 1888, showing the arch to the livery stables and the Georgian glazing bars in the bay windows. The short-lived Plough beerhouse is the house with bay windows on the left, and the barn on the upper side is now 7 Dyer's Hill.

The Rose and Crown was another inn sign marking the end of the Wars of the Roses by the marriage of Henry Tudor to Elizabeth of York in 1486 – they are said to have first met in Wychwood Forest while hunting. Our Rose and Crown was a charming 'L' shaped building on the corner of Church Street and Market Street. The earliest written mention of it is in 1688 in the deeds of the old Barclay's Bank. It was one of the four main inns in the market place, and successive landlords looked after the building well. Photographs taken before 1906 show a Georgian façade with contemporary sash windows. But private ownership gave way to takeovers by breweries, and when a small jeweller's shop in the Church Street wing caught fire on 11 September 1905, Clinch and Co. Witney, seized the opportunity to demolish the (undamaged) Rose and Crown and rebuild. During the demolition the party wall between the Market Street frontage and Benjamin Luker's Boot and Shoe Emporium (later Barclay's Bank) fell down including his fireplaces and chimneys. Compensation was demanded, and paid. But we are left with a very boring building facing Market Street and a purpose-built butcher's shop in Church Street faced

The attractive Church Street front of the Rose and Crown (right) before 1905.

with shiny brown and white bricks usually associated with gents' lavatories (the white ones have now been given a cement coat). A purpose-built post office, now Chancellor's estate agents, was also incorporated between Benjamin Luker's and the diminished Rose and Crown. In the 1970s it suddenly changed its name to The Charlbury Tavern, spelt out in scarlet plastic letters eighteen inches high. Luckily, new owners went back to the old name in the 1980s.

The Bull, once in a commanding position opposite the medieval Market House in the centre of the widest part of the Market Place, must refer to the barbaric custom of bull baiting. Bulldogs, bull mastiffs and bull terriers were set onto an animal tethered to an iron ring in the wall for the enjoyment of onlookers. According to Jesse Clifford's memoirs, the last bull baiting took place in 1820 on the Playing Close.

The Elizabethan building in Thames Street (earlier known as Dog Street) opposite Nineacres Lane was probably an inn for centuries. Variously called The Greyhound (one of the supporters on Queen

The Market Street front of the Rose and Crown, before 1905.

Elizabeth's coat of arms); The Talbot, a large white hunting dog with long ears (badge of the Earls of Shrewsbury); The Spotted Dog (a Talbot with spots, that is, a Dalmatian); or just The Dog, it must have incorporated Armada Cottage, and possibly a balancing wing at the other end. The large yard is now occupied by Cotswold View and Thames Gardens – formerly Dog Yard crammed with the poorest slum dwellings in the late 19th century. It ceased to be licensed in 1927, having escaped 'modernisation' by Hall's Oxford Brewery in 1914 by the outbreak of war.

The Royal Oak in Church Street must date from about 1660 and refer to King Charles II's sojourn in the Boscobel oak tree in 1651. Charlbury

The Talbot Inn, Thames Street.

had many close links with the House of Stuart. This inn became a coffee house in 1879, and the inn sign is now in the Museum.

Of the rather more ephemeral beerhouses, several ceased to offer refreshment when their original owners departed. The Masons' Arms in 2 and 3 Brown's Lane was run by the Kibble family from c.1814 to c.1859. The Glovers' Arms in Market Street became The Oxford Arms in 1858 when Hall's Oxford Brewery bought it (it is now known as Oxford House), ceased to be licensed in 1915 and became the Midland Bank. I am not sure when the present façade was put on, but in 1898 the wife of George Forrest, the landlord, hung herself from the stairs to the top floor which housed the New Friendly Society Clubroom. Probably the unin- spired frontage was the work of Hall's Oxford Brewery.

The Plough on Dyer's Hill was only a beerhouse when the farmyard (now occupied by Victoria Terrace) and double-fronted farm house above the large green doors were occupied by the Smith family in the 1880s. The Queen's Own in Church Lane was run as a beerhouse and tramps' lodging house in the 1850s and 60s by Thomas Wells, band- master of D Troop, Queen's Own Oxfordshire Yeomanry Cavalry

Regiment. Queen Adelaide, wife of William IV had graciously permitted the Royal appellation in 1835.

The Bear in Sheep Street (now Providence House) became another travellers' lodging house when it was run by Mrs Martha Ruddle in the 1870s. It was handed on to George Octavius Gomm, a retired policeman, in 1888. The orchard behind the building was bought by Vernon Watney in 1902 and given to the Oxfordshire County Council Education Committee as a playground for the Council School.

What is now known as The Farmers in Sheep Street was formerly The Railway Arms, a name obviously inspired by the opening of the OWW Railway in 1853. Possibly it was called The Three Horseshoes before that. There is an interesting folk tale about this beerhouse. In 1811 John Gondoux, a widower, the landlord, was thought to have hung himself, and he was buried on Banbury Hill at a crossroads, without religious rites. But his neighbours dug him up at dead of night, put him in a coffin and buried him in the churchyard. Many years later an old woman on her deathbed confessed that she had seen Gondoux's son-in-law climb a ladder and enter the bedroom where he strangled his father-in-law and made it look like suicide. According to the (rather sketchy) church registers, John Gondoux had one son-in-law, Thomas Carpenter. By an extraordinary coincidence, a descendant of John Gondoux got in touch me via the internet, and it was interesting to discover that there are descendants of this transient inhabitant still alive in England!

The Swan, a cottage now within the grounds of Lee Place, was a beerhouse in 1779. Lee's Rest was also licensed from 1777 to 1800, to catch travellers to and from Woodstock before the new route for the Turnpike Road was made.

The Ball, sometimes the Golden Ball, was housed in the half-timbered Market House in the centre of the old Market Place. The last recorded landlord, following on from William Poole, Mary Poole and Isaac Fletcher, was William Milton in 1801. The Victuallers Recognizances for 1803 and 1804 are missing, but sometime during these two years, the licence was given up.

The landlord of the Marlborough Arms in Park Street in 1848 was

The half-timbered Market House was completely disguised under a stucco coat (**above**) after it ceased to be The Golden Ball. After the stocks were removed, a succession of ironmongers used the space under the roof as an outside showroom. The roof was dismantled (**below**) in 1871 as a traffic hazard, and because it made the ironmonger's shop dark.

Thomas Lay, followed in the 1860s by the Drapers, who were black-smiths. The Duke of Marlborough's Trustees bought a large amount of land in Charlbury after 1744, and probably lip service was paid to the landowner by naming an inn after him.

The lists of licensed victuallers authorised by local JPs to sell ale or other liquors in an orderly way cover the years from 1753 to 1822. Fifteen landlords are named for 1753 in Charlbury, but until 1779 the names of their houses are not given – which is frustrating. In 1774 two sureties of £10 annually had to be provided, very often by the landlord of the inn in question and the landlord of a nearby inn. The money would be forfeit if the use of unjust measures was proved or if gambling had taken place. In that year nine landlords were named. By 1801 it seems that only inns with full licences to sell spirits as well as beer were listed – Ball, Bell, Bull, Rose and Crown, Star, White Hart, Talbot and Royal Oak – beerhouses were not included. Few landlords could live on the profit from the inn, and most had other occupations. The Bell and White Hart were also posting inns with livery stables. The inns still with us today in 2000 are The Bell, The Bull, The Rose and Crown and The Farmers, all of them free houses.

When many national breweries merged after the last war, Ind Coope, owners of The Bell, were taken over by Allied Breweries. The policy of Allied was to get rid of tenant landlords and put in managers. The manager put in charge of The Bell came from London, had a passion for juke boxes, wore a bowler hat when behind the bar, and played the spoons to entertain his customers. He also used petrol to light the fire in the bar. Called in to put out the subsequent chimney fire, the local firemen, many of whom had enjoyed drinking there before the tenant landlord was sacked, assiduously poured water down the flue from the roof until there was nearly a foot of sooty water in the bar. The manager left, and Allied sold The Bell to Lord Rotherwick. Since then, there has been a succession of tenants, but none has been able to recapture the old atmosphere of a truly classless 'local'.

J. A. Bowl's shop in Church Street decorated for the coronation of George V in 1911. He won first prize.

A new century

Queen Victoria died on 22 January 1901 at Osborne House, Isle of Wight. On the day of her funeral, 4 February, a strong southerly wind blew and Charlbury people were convinced that the thunder they heard for three hours was really the sound of naval guns at Spithead firing a farewell salute.

Queen Victoria's death in 1901 emphasised the feeling of *fin de siècle*, and things were further upset when the Coronation of Edward VII had to be postponed because of the new King's trend-setting appendectomy. Edward's reign was marked in Charlbury by opportunities for the towns-people to 'better themselves'. The County Council arranged evening classes in reading, writing, arithmetic, cookery, needlework and gardening. Meetings of the Manchester Order of Oddfellows, the Wychwood branch of the Ancient Order of Foresters, the YMCA and YWCA, and the Church Lads' Brigade (formed by the Rev. J. D. Payne, who continued to give it his whole-hearted support, especially when the Charlbury branch competed in 'skirmishing' contests) were regular events reported in the *Oxford Times*. The year was always punctuated by the Church festivals, and in between there were socials, concerts, sports, debates and lectures with lantern slides. Lady Margaret Watney (daughter of the 5th Earl of Portsmouth) knew what was expected of the Lady of the Manor, and never failed to give enthusiastic support to the Red Cross, local Nursing Association, school events, Horticultural Society and any other local project.

The Coronation of George V in 1911 was a well-documented affair for Charlbury. A competition for the best-decorated shop or house produced a wonderful array of designs, which were photographed. Mr Bowl won first prize for his shop in Church Street, now known as Baileys. The fancy dress procession was led by Mr. G. J. Jones JP dressed in a pith helmet

Leading the Coronation Parade in 1911 are Mr G. J. Jones in pith helmet and safari suit; Rev. Julius Delmege Payne, Vicar 1903–1939; and H. G. Elkington, Clerk to the Parish Council.

The Mill Cut at the bottom of Pound Hill before it silted up. It was used as a village pond for watering cattle, soaking wooden cart wheels to keep the iron tyres on, and as a mooring for punts.

The total immersion of a Baptist in the Mill Cut at the old bathing place, 1914.

and safari suit. He was a master baker who had won a Gold Medal for Hovis bread, a District Councillor, Chairman of the Parish Council, a school manager, a trustee on all the local charity trusts, and a staunch Wesleyan. He gave the bit of land down Water Lane (now occupied by the Canoe Club huts) as a bathing place for the town. This was fenced off with corrugated iron sheets and one or two changing cubicles were put up. For a time aquatic sports were the fashion, and it was the site of the total immersion baptism of four Baptists in 1914.

The popularity of the Miniature Rifle Club (behind the Friends' Meeting House in Market St), the increase in volunteers for the Territorial Army and possibly the 'skirmishing' contests held by the Church Lads' Brigade, cast a shadow over the future.

The 1914-18 war had a profound effect on rural communities. The heart-rending accounts in the *Oxford Times* of military tribunals held at Chipping Norton to decide who was indispensable to the local agriculture and way of life in Charlbury are difficult reading. Luckily the profligate squandering of the common people of England by exclusively stupid and hidebound army top brass wasn't copied in the 1939-45 war. In 1928

The council houses built on Enstone Road in 1920.

everyone had a vote (except peers, felons and lunatics) but today some people don't realise what an effort went into the fight for universal suffrage.

After the Great War, houses were needed for the returning warriors. The District Council built four pairs of houses in Enstone Road on Nine Acres in 1920. A gap was left in the middle of the row for a road to serve the proposed estate in Nine Acres. Luckily this never materialised, and the remainder of Nine Acres was given to the town as a playing field.

The ancient ritual of beating the bounds of the parish was revived in 1924, during which the tragic drowning of two children and a young woman occurred. The 75th anniversary in 1999 brought together one of the rescuers and one of those he rescued.

When Chadlington was disreputably included in Charlbury parish by Eynsham Abbey in the 13th century, I wonder whether the young men of the parish were led all the way round the perimeter, being beaten by the elders at various spots so that they would be sure not to forget. The place where the overladen punt overturned was referred to as the Devil's Elbow, a few yards upstream from the beginning of the Mill Cut at Jubilee Bridge. On Thomas Pride's 1761 map the field on the Charlbury side of the river is called Hunting Bridge Meadow, so perhaps in earlier times the bound

The funeral of the two children drowned while beating the bounds in 1924.

beaters could have walked across it. There were 30-year gaps in the 19th century, and it is only since the Parish/Town Council began to organise it that the boundary walk has been done on an annual basis again.

Between the wars, life went on in a quiet way, with plenty of local shops and local jobs available. In 1928 J. A. Bowl, whose family had run the provision shop at the bottom of Church Street for 81 years, sold it to Frank Bailey of Thame, who bred Great Danes. That year, too, the Post Office moved along Market Street to The Elms (now the ladies' hairdresser) because more room was needed for the (manual) telephone exchange. Five years later, Mr and Mrs Davis, the sub-postmaster and mistress, retired and Mr Mapperley from Brize Norton took over. Mr and Mrs Davis, who had been here since 1917, were presented with an oak coal-scuttle, a silver-mounted sugar caster and an eight-pint copper kettle suitably engraved.

Ditchley Park also changed hands. In 1933 Lord Dillon died and the estate was bought by Ronald Lambert Tree MP, aged 37, with a wife and two sons. He also owned Kelmarsh Hall, Northants, a house in Queen Anne's Gate, and an estate in Virginia, USA. He had enough money to

The Priory, where Eynsham Abbey's bailiff lived and where Manorial Courts were held until 1539. It is probably as old as the church. It was never a priory.

modernise the house, adding the number of bathrooms considered essential by Americans.

In 1934 Captain J. H. Waller died aged 94. He had lived in Charlbury since 1879, first at Lee Place and from 1905 at The Priory. (I think it may have been he who misnamed the house.) He it was who founded the Charlbury Volunteer Fire Brigade in 1881, and assiduously organised fund-raising events for it in the grounds of Lee Place. But by 1927 (he was then 87) when the new Fire Station in Brown's Lane and new statutes for the Brigade were in operation, others had taken over. In 1932 he sued the Fire Brigade for possession of the portrait of General Buller, now in the Museum, and the Brigade counter-claimed for a silver cup presented by his daughter, Elizabeth (Mrs Bevil Smithe). Neither side won. In 1934 the Fire Engine wheels were changed from solid to pneumatic tyres.

Before the Brown's Lane fire station was built in 1927, the old Blind House (or lock-up) on the Playing Close was altered to house the horse-drawn fire engine.

In 1933 there was an acute water shortage, but it wasn't until 1937 that Chipping Norton Rural District Council agreed to buy the Charlbury Waterworks Co. for £3,500, knowing the improvements and extensions would cost £4,500. For some reason they demolished Charlbury Mill in 1937.

In 1934 Samuel Gibson Shilson, the wool stapler, died of peritonitis, aged 72. He and W. A. Albright had bought Nine Acres and presented it to the town as a recreation ground. A pitch for hockey, two for football, a tennis court and a bowling green were levelled in about 1951. The hard surface play area was completed in 1995.

Another very important figure left Charlbury in July 1935. Lady Margaret Watney, who had given unstintingly of her time, support, encouragement, money and garden produce since she and her husband bought Cornbury Park in 1902, bowed gracefully out and moved to Williamstrip Park, Hatherop, leaving a clear field for her daughter-in-law,

Charlbury water mill in about 1900. There had been a mill on this site since before 1363.

Christina Nelson, who had been married to Oliver Watney by the Archbishop of Canterbury in December 1934. In 1926 Parliament abolished copyhold tenure, and when Oliver Watney inherited Cornbury in 1928 he wrote to all his copyhold tenants offering, for a small sum, to change copyhold to freehold tenure in the Manor of Charlbury. The only rights he retained as Lord of the Manor were the mineral rights.

During the 1939-45 war, Cornbury Park became an Ordnance Depot, packed to the edges with everything the Army required, a temptation in times of shortage that some found impossible to resist. Ditchley, the home of Ronald Tree, was a refuge for Winston Churchill at weekends when the moon was full; his minders felt that German bombers might target Downing Street or Chequers. One or two bombs did drop harmlessly in a field near Lee's Rest; you can still see the craters they made.

Charlbury was a reception area for many evacuees from the East End of London, and being a billeting officer was a most unpopular job. The Durham Light Infantry Regiment were stationed here, and left their mark

These two Grade II listed cottages in Market Street were illegally demolished one bank holiday weekend in the 1970s by a greedy grocer, who was drummed out of town. The present Post Office now occupies the site.

on a metal plate let into the bar of The Bell Hotel. Dad's Army, Land Girls, ARP Wardens, Plane Spotters (the Royal Observer Corps), Fire Fighters – the local volunteer brigade was taken over by the National Fire Service as soon as war was declared – all had representatives here. An air raid siren or 'Moaning Minnie' was fixed on a pole at the fire station in

Brown's Lane. Everyone Dug for Victory, and the Women's Institute canned or jammed all possible wild fruit or surplus garden produce. Ration books for food and identity cards were issued to every civilian, and soon clothes were rationed too, when the U boats sank so many of our merchant ships. Petrol coupons were almost unobtainable, unless one was doing essential war work. *ITMA*, local dances for the troops and visits to the cinema helped to keep morale up and so did Winston Churchill. It was a great surprise to many when Clement Attlee won the 1945 General Election, but the 1939-45 war brought about a mini revolution. The 'lower' classes rose and the 'upper' classes levelled off. Soon nearly everyone in Charlbury had a car, which enabled the men to work in Oxford at Pressed Steel or the Cowley works. Local shops closed as wives also had full-time jobs and shopped at the new supermarkets. New estates sprang up here and the population doubled in the 1960s and 70s. Because every family owned a car – and sometimes every member of every family – traffic became a problem in the medieval township. A one-way system was implemented in 1976 and country lanes – The Slade, for example – were widened and became mini racetracks. The 30 mph speed limit was imposed in 1974 and double yellow lines were painted in 1981. Charlbury became a Conservation Area in 1974 and – through the efforts of Mrs Juler, our County Councillor – part of the Cotswolds Area of Outstanding Natural Beauty in November 1986.

Because of the speed at which new houses were built and occupied by strangers, there was a certain amount of friction between Charlburians and what were dubbed 'white settlers', but those incomers who quietly join local societies and offer their, often skilled, help are soon felt to be assets to the community. Ex-city dwellers who try to change things the moment they arrive are not so welcome.

But Charlbury is a friendly town, and I count myself very fortunate to live here.

Bibliography

Allport, D.H., *Ramsden, the story of a Wychwood Village* (1965)

Barracuda Guide to County History Vol.II. Oxfordshire, Geoffrey Stevenson (1977)

Beckinsale, R. & M., *The English Heartland* (1980)

Beesley, A., *History of Banbury* (1841)

Brewer, J.N., *Topographical & Historical Description of Oxfordshire* (1810)

Clifford, Jesse, *My Reminiscences of Charlbury* (1892)

Corbett, Hon. Elsie, *History of Spelsbury* (1962)

Davies, G.J., *A Farewell Letter to the Parishioners of Charlbury* (1857)

Delderfield, E.R., *British Inn Signs* (1965)

Ditchfield, P.H. (ed), *Memorials of old Oxfordshire* (1903)

Domesday Book Oxenfordscire, Morris, J. (ed) Phillimore (1978)

Gelling, M., *Place Names of Oxfordshire*, 2 vols (1953)

Gretton, M. Sturge, *A Corner of the Cotswolds* (1913)

Harris, Mollie, *Wychwood: the Secret Cotswold Forest* (1991)

Henderson, M. Sturge, *Three Centuries in North Oxfordshire* (1902)

Hill, Robert, *A Short History of Charlbury* (1975)

Hoskins, W.G., *The Making of the English Landscape* (1955, 1988)

Jessup, Mary, *A History of Oxfordshire* (1975)

Jordan, Rev. J., *The History of Enstone* (1857)

Kibble, J., *Historical & other notes on Charlbury* (1927)

> *Historical & other notes on Wychwood Forest & many of its border places* (1928). Reprinted by The Wychwood Press as *Wychwood Forest and Its Border Places* (1999)

> *Charming Charlbury* (1930). Reprinted by The Wychwood Press (1999)

Marshall, R.M., *Oxfordshire Byways* (1949)

Morris, C. (ed), *The Journeys of Celia Fiennes* (1949)

Oxfordshire Records Society, Weinstock (ed), *Hearth Tax Returns 1665*

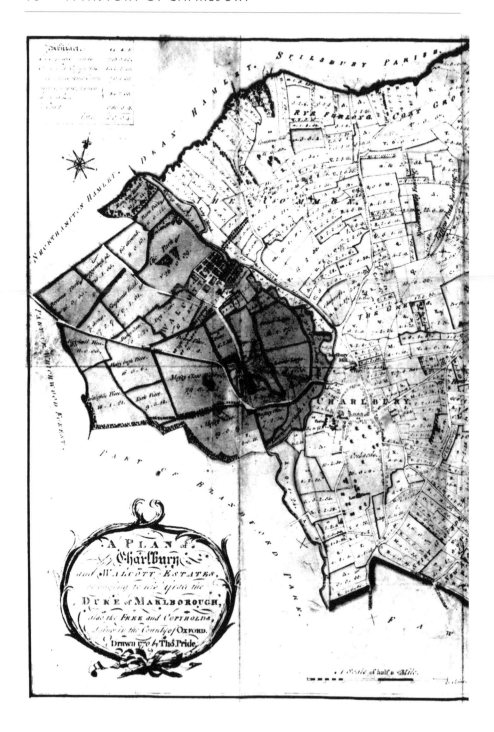

Thomas Pride's map of Charlbury and Walcot, drawn for the Duke of Marlborough in 1770.

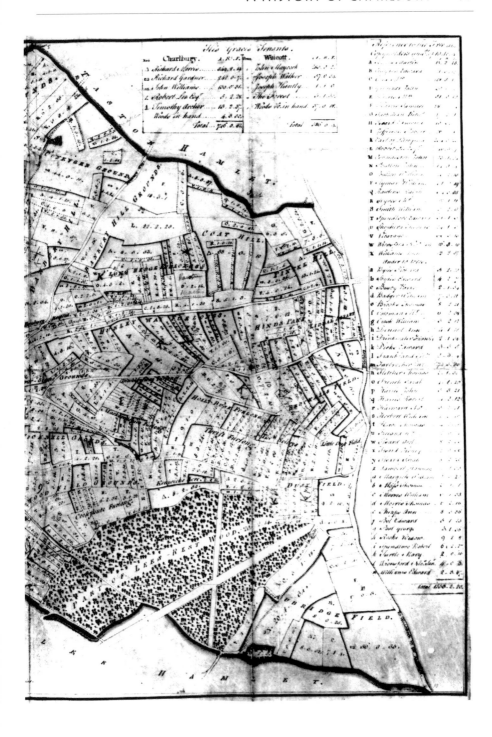

Oxfordshire Records Society, Weinstock (ed), *Hearth Tax Returns 1665* (1940)

Payne, J.D., *Notes on the History of Charlbury* (1935)

Plot, Robert, *Natural History of Oxfordshire* (1675)

Pumphrey, Caroline Westcombe, *The Charlbury of Our Childhood 1845-1860* (1990)

Salter, H.E. (ed), *Cartularies of Eynsham Abbey*, 2 vols (1907)

Schumer, Beryl, *Wychwood; The Evolution of a Wooded Landscape* (2nd edition, 1999)

Victoria County History, Vol.I (1902)

   Vol.II (1907)

   Vol.X (1970) Charlbury in Banbury Hundred

   (1991) Wootton Hundred

Watney, Vernon James, *Cornbury and the Forest of Wychwood* (1910)

Wickham-Steed, Violet, *Wychwood Forest: Its History and Management* (ms in Oxfordshire County Museum)

Appendix

A geological view of the history of Charlbury

Professor Geoffrey Walton

1 · INTRODUCTION

The Town of Charlbury lies on the east bank of the River Evenlode, just above that section of the valley known to geologists as the Evenlode Gorge. Most of the solid, bedrock strata comprise limestones of the Jurassic Period but important clays and more sandy strata are also present. In earlier geological times Coal Measure deposits were formed in the area and lie deep beneath the Town. During the recent geological past, including glacial and interglacial episodes, higher and lower level gravels were deposited possibly with several episodes of rapidly outwashed gravels from large deposits of glacial debris further up the Evenlode Valley. Frozen ground conditions such as exist in Siberia today are known to have occurred in Charlbury as recently as a few tens of thousands of years ago.

The sequence of strata and overlying superficial deposits from top to bottom is summarised in the list below. It is based on revision mapping by the British Geological Survey in the 1970s and later publications as follows:

Superficial deposits:
- Alluvium also glacial disturbed superficial and bedrock strata) Recent
- Upper Thames Formation – river gravels   )
- Northern Drift Formation – high level gravels) Quarternary
)

Bedrock formations:
- Oxford Clay   )   )
- Kellaways Formation   ) Not present within)
- Cornbrash Formation   ) parish boundary   )
- Forest Marble Formation   )
- White Limestone Formation   )
- Hampen Formation*   )
- Taynton Limestone Formation*   ) Jurassic
- Charlbury Formation*   )
- Sharp's Hill Formation*   )
- Chipping Norton Limestone Formation   )
- Clypeus Grit   )
- Upper Lias   )
- Middle Lias and Marlstone Rock Bed   )
- Lower Lias (partly concealed)   )
- Triassic (concealed)
- Upper Coal Measures (concealed)

* These formations contain occasional 'Stonesfield Slate' type beds.

History of geological investigations in Charlbury

The earliest geological investigations in the Charlbury area were prob-ably undertaken by William Smith, a mineral surveyor, born at Churchill, who worked for a time at Daylesford House just over the county boundary. Smith, known as the 'Father of British Geology', produced the first geological map of Britain in 1815 and a little later in 1820 a Geological Map of Oxfordshire (on a John Cary base plan) showing a significant number of geological formations near the Town. Amazing though his achievements were, his map shows much of the Town lying on what he describes as 'Blue Marl' and only the upper part of the parish as having 'Under and Upper Oolite Rocks'. Smith is also credited with first identifying the Forest Marble (named after Wychwood Forest), his plan showing Stonesfield Slates and Forest Marble grouped together.

The Geological Survey now known as the British Geological Survey (BGS) first systematically mapped the Charlbury area in the 1850s and noted the occurrence of ironstone at Fawler. These investigations led directly to the working of ironstone by opencast and underground means at Fawler. Towards the end of the nineteenth century a number of boreholes were drilled to enlarge and deepen Charlbury's water supply.

Throughout the twentieth century there has been much academic interest in the origin of the high level Triassic (Bunter) gravels, such as those found around Gordon House off Woody Lane. Some regarded them as residual deposits from a glacier which moved down the Evenlode Valley as far as the south of the county and others as river gravels associated with a pre-glacial River Thames. In the middle of the last century the Gas Council drilled a deep borehole in the old gasworks near the railway station and the National Coal Board and others drilled boreholes outside the parish boundary from which it may be inferred that coal bearing strata lie 250-300m beneath the Town.

Finally, over the last three decades there have been a number of site investigations for proposed developments or following settlement problems which have provided interesting information on shallow ground conditions. Boreholes continue to be drilled for water and provide further information. Quite recently investigations have shown that the Stonesfield Slates, which are used for roofing many Charlbury buildings, are not restricted as previously supposed to a small area round the village of Stonesfield, but lie within the strata which may be seen in Charlbury Quarry. In consequence, a new geological formation has been recognised which includes some of the tilestones known as 'Stonesfield Slate'; this formation has been named the Charlbury Formation.

Geology and the development of the Town

Like most small and larger settlements along the Evenlode Valley, Charlbury has been located by Romans, Saxons and more recent settlers just above the major spring line in the North Cotswolds. Hereabouts the

Clypeus Grit, a variably rubbly and massive oolitic limestone together with the overlying Chipping Norton Limestone, form a largely unconfined aquifer perched on top of the Upper Lias Clay.

The development of Charlbury has not been influenced by mineral workings in the way that Stonesfield, Fawler and Leafield were with the mining of roofing tiles and ironstone and the working of pottery clays. However, it has for centuries (until the late 1990s) provided stone of high quality from the Chipping Norton Limestone and other limestones, latterly from the Town Quarry. Previously it provided its own materials for road building, including kerbstones until the start of the last century and some of the stone was suitable for dimensional use. Local limestone kerbs were still in place in Church Street until the 1980s. The character of the heart of Charlbury as defined by its older buildings is still shaped by stone which came from within its boundaries.

In the late 1800s a firm, variously called the Charlbury Brick Co and Bolton and Partners Ltd, made bricks in Fawler from the Upper and Middle Lias Clays for a few years which were used in a number of buildings in the Town. Natural stone in most new buildings in Charlbury comes from Gloucestershire (unless it is reconstituted stone as in most of the more recent estates). However, the Chipping Norton Limestone is still worked between Churchill and Sarsden and some of this stone has been used in the last ten years for renovation work in the Town.

The geology of the parish has only limited influence on the Town today since most matters such as ground conditions, building materials and water resources can either be resolved by appropriate engineering or brought in from outside. Remaining items of current or recent interest which have a bearing on local geology include the locally high radon gas levels, waste disposal and the influence of groundwater and related environmental issues on development control.

2 · BEDROCK STRATA

Deep bedrock

Details of the North Oxfordshire Coalfield were published in the 1960s and 1970s. The deepest boreholes drilled in the area show **Upper Coal Measure** strata (Westphalian) under much of West Oxfordshire. The strata comprise mainly reddened mudstones, siltstones and sandstones, with relatively little coal. The Burford and Witney Coal Groups, which contain these strata, lie more than 250m beneath Charlbury (more than 160m below sea level); about 8 coal seams more than 0.6m thick are inferred to be present. Boreholes elsewhere in the county show thicker coals at lower levels. The quality is low with high ash and sulphur contents and relatively low calorific values. It is unlikely to be worked or considered for gasification in the foreseeable future. One of the issues relating to its viability is that the groundwater at depth is saline, probably from the overlying Triassic rocks which are known elsewhere in England to contain salt rich beds.

Above the Carboniferous strata, Triassic sandstones and mudstones occur. The sandstones known as the **Bromsgrove Sandstone Formation** are about 20m thick in the Charlbury area and are followed by 50m of red mudstones and siltstones with thin veins of gypsum. This part of the sequence is known as the **Mercia Mudstone** and is used as raw material for engineering bricks elsewhere in England. At the top of the Trias there are approximately 20m of dark grey to green mudstones and siltstones with thinner sandstones. Much of the Triassic strata is thought to be non-marine or brackish in origin, but towards the end of Triassic times a very widely spread thin limestone occurs known as the White Lias (or the Langport Member of the Lilstock Formation). This limestone includes marine fossils and is about 2m thick beneath Charlbury. It marks the onset of marine conditions that existed for most of the time during which the Lower and Middle Jurassic strata outcropping around Charlbury were deposited. The White Lias occurs about 120m beneath Charlbury Station but outcrops nearby in South Warwickshire where it has been used in characteristic pale grey eighteenth and nineteenth century buildings.

The White Lias is followed by about 110m of **Lower Lias** strata which are predominantly clay with thin impure, but highly persistent limestone bands. At Southam in Warwickshire this clay was used with imported chalk for cement manufacture. The top 10 to 15m of Lower Lias Clay is poorly exposed beneath alluvium in the floors of the Evenlode near Charlbury and the side valleys, but is thought to have previously been exposed in the old clay pits at Fawler from which the Charlbury Brick Co worked its raw materials.

Exposed bedrock

The Lias Strata

Above the Lower Lias clays with thin limestones lie the **Middle Lias** silts and clays followed by the **Marlstone Rock Bed** (ironstone). The silts and clays are about 10 to 15m thick (based on boreholes) but, like the Lower Lias Clays, are poorly exposed. They have been found at the surface along the lowest sections of Clarke's Bottom and in the deep site investigation trial trenches in Blakes Yard (now Tanners Court). Here the silty clays are much thinner, no more than 2m, probably due to the squeezing out of the clays by valley bulging (see section on Superficial Geology below).

The Marlstone Rock Bed is quite thin near Charlbury, being only 1.5 to 2.5m thick in recent gas pipeline excavations west of the Priory and in Tanners Court respectively and about 3m thick in boreholes drilled along the Ditchley Road. It was mined opencast and underground in the latter half of the nineteenth century at Fawler and more extensively by opencast methods in the country between Hook Norton and Bloxham in the last century. Known at Fawler as 'Blenheim iron ore', it was used in iron and steel works at Brymbo in North Wales from which area it is thought coal was brought for the former gas works which was located west of the railway station. The Fawler mines were worked from 1858 to 1866 and 1880 to 1886. Underground workings lie north-east of the road at Fawler and a collapse in one of the tunnels is thought to have led to its eventual closure.

The ironstone, often rusty or reddish brown in colour, is typical of a low

quality (20-30% iron) with a 10-20% calcium oxide content. The main iron
bearing minerals are chamosite and siderite. The lower part of the Marlstone
Rock Bed includes a significant phosphate content (as the mineral apatite)
sometimes in excess of 1.0%, mainly as phosphatic nodules which contain
low concentrations of uranium. Radon is a decay product of U238 in the
form of a gas which can migrate to the ground surface. Radon is thought to
be carcinogenic and may account for 5% of deaths from lung cancer in the
UK. That part of Charlbury which lies immediately above the outcrop of the
Marlstone Rock Bed is an area of medium to high risk from radon gas and
new properties in such areas may be required to accommodate special foundation measures to avoid accumulation of the gas within the buildings;
fortunately there are few such buildings.

Large parts of North Oxfordshire, including land around Great Tew,
have planning permission to work the ironstone. It is no longer used in
iron and steel making in Britain today, having a higher than desirable
phosphorus content, but it is used in places as a source of fill materials,
walling stone and occasionally for high density concrete aggregates.
Buildings in Charlbury seldom have Marlstone Rock Bed in the
stonework, but some is included in part of the north side of the parish
church. As a building material it is much weaker and more frost susceptible than other local stones as may be seen when visiting villages north of
Charlbury built with this stone.

At the top of the Lias strata lies the **Upper Lias Clay**. This occurs at
lower levels around the Town and is usually a blue/grey clay hereabouts
with ironstone nodules in the lower part. Away from valley sides the
Upper Lias Clay is about 10m thick in boreholes, but it is commonly
squeezed out or covered by cambered overlying limestones in and near
valleys. The waterworks borehole (no longer in use) north of Nine Acres
Lane showed about 5.8m of Upper Lias Clay and a slightly reduced thickness was computed in the Tanners Court investigations. The British
Geological Survey record an outcrop thickness of about 3m in Clarke's
Bottom. The clay locally appears to be an aquiclude which leads to water
in the overlying limestones issuing at a quite obvious spring line. This
spring line feeds the brook which crosses Sandford Slade as well as that in

Clarke's Bottom. It possibly also contributes to the spring in the garden of the old Toll House at the bottom of Dyer's Hill. Most older wells in Charlbury were dug to just above the top of the Upper Lias Clay to intercept groundwater perched on the clay, e.g. Bay Well, the Cyder Well in Cornbury Park, the formerly important Town well in Fishers Lane and water supplies to houses such as Evencroft and Rook's Nest on the Spelsbury Road. The former brewery in Park Street, recently converted to houses, would have used water from this aquifer.

Middle Jurassic

Previously the Middle Jurassic was subdivided into the Inferior Oolite and the Great Oolite. The sequence of strata near Charlbury is subdivided on lithostratigraphic grounds into eight formations which are found within the parish boundary. The lowest five formations have been exposed at some time in the Town Quarry. From top to bottom they are:
- Taynton Limestone Formation
- Charlbury Formation
- Sharp's Hill Formation
- Chipping Norton Limestone Formation
- Clypeus Grit

The **Clypeus Grit**, which in Charlbury sits on the Upper Lias Clays, is the only section of the Inferior Oolite deposited in the area. This formation is named after a characteristic fossil *Clypeus Plotii*, an echinoid first reported by Robert Plot in 1676 in his book *The Natural History of Oxfordshire*. Elsewhere in the Cotswolds, north-west of Charlbury, limestones up to 90m thick occur below the Clypeus Grit which are widely used for dimension stone (sawn or otherwise dressed stone for use in ashlar or quoins and walling stone, nowadays typically sawn and split). The Clypeus Grit is a member of the Salperton Limestone Formation. It is a cream to pale brown limestone, massive and oolitic in places, but often rubbly at outcrop and with occasional bands of clay up to 100mm thick. In the Town Quarry about 5m of the estimated 10 to 12m of the formation were visible before restoration. The lower part which is more rubbly was not worked, but is exposed on the north-eastern side of the railway cutting near the road to Cornbury House as well as in recent trenches in Fisher's Lane and near Sandford Mount.

The **Chipping Norton Limestone**, from which many of the older buildings in Charlbury are constructed, is exposed in its entirety in the restored Town Quarry. It is about 6-8m thick and may be distinguished from the limestones above and below by its sandy as well as oolitic nature. It shows all the features of shallow water deposition with ripple marks and banks of shell debris. The sandy nature of the rock, together with its density makes it a good building stone which is less susceptible to frost damage than many other Cotswold stones. Most of the upper part of the Town stands on Chipping Norton Limestone which was worked in a number of old quarries between the Ditchley Road and Hundley Way, and at the former small quarry at Conygree Farm.

In the Town Quarry the contact with the overlying **Sharp's Hill Formation** is quite obvious. The dark grey and sometimes peaty carbonaceous clays stand out distinctly from the overlying limestones of the Charlbury Formation and the Chipping Norton Limestone below. The formation is about 3m thick and includes thin shelly limestones. Oyster shells are abundant and plant debris is found in some of the clay bands. The deposit is thought to be indicative of brackish water and some of the fossils are of fresh water origin. The clays and limestone bands were formed in shallow water conditions. They act as an aquiclude and therefore groundwater is often perched above the Sharp's Hill Formation, a situation found in a water well drilled in the 1980s at Banbury Hill Farm. The Sharp's Hill Formation is the lateral equivalent of the Lower Fullers Earth in North Gloucestershire. A very similar sequence of strata to that in the Town Quarry can for example be seen at Huntsmans Quarry near Naunton, west of Stow.

For many years it was assumed that the Stonesfield Slate was a separate geological unit which was laterally equivalent to the Sharp's Hill Formation. Investigations in the early 1990s showed that the Sharp's Hill Formation lies beneath the strata in Stonesfield from which the roofing tiles were worked until the early years of the last century. Further investigations have shown that the Stonesfield Slates (which are not slates *sensu stricto*, but thinly laminated calcareous fine grained sandstones) occur at a number of levels in the local geological sequence from the Sharp's Hill Formation up to the Hampen Formation. Most of the slate workings appear to have been in the Taynton Limestone Formation. Hence 'Stonesfield Slate' is a rock type and cannot be used to identify (correlate) the geological formation from which it comes. It has been of considerable interest in the past because of land derived fossils which include reptiles and early mammals as well as insects and plants. Most of the fossils are marine again indicating shallow water conditions of sedimentation. The removal of Stonesfield Slate as a specific geological unit to a rock type which occurs at different levels in the strata helps to account for its occurrence and previous workings at other places such as Fulwell and Filkins.

Above the Sharp's Hill Formation Charlbury's Town Quarry shows 4.8m of thin bedded impure oolitic and sandy, shelly limestones with a thin Stonesfield Slate type calcareous sandstone at its base. This strata has been recently designated the **Charlbury Formation** and has been found to extend as far as Cirencester and Swindon. It is clearly distinguished from the overlying Taynton Limestone Formation by the latter's coarse grained and cross bedded nature with a paucity of whole fossils.

The base of the **Taynton Limestone Formation** is also exposed in the Town Quarry. Although used in the past at Taynton for dimension stone (at Lee's Quarry) it was rarely sufficiently massive at Charlbury for such use, being suitable only for fill or dry walling. It was previously quarried on the east side of Banbury Hill Road where the strata dips gently to the south. This limestone is about 7-10m thick and in the fields north and east of Charlbury its upper surface is distinguished by brashy limestone rubble with many oyster fragments which come from the base of the overlying Hampen Formation.

The **Hampen Formation** is a banded unit about 6m thick comprising shelly clays and marls with marly and sandy limestone bands and fissile calcareous sandstones (Stonesfield Slate type beds). It produces a heavy, sticky clay soil which is apparent when walking from the Town Quarry to Dustfield Farm and also along Hundley Way near its junction with the Salt

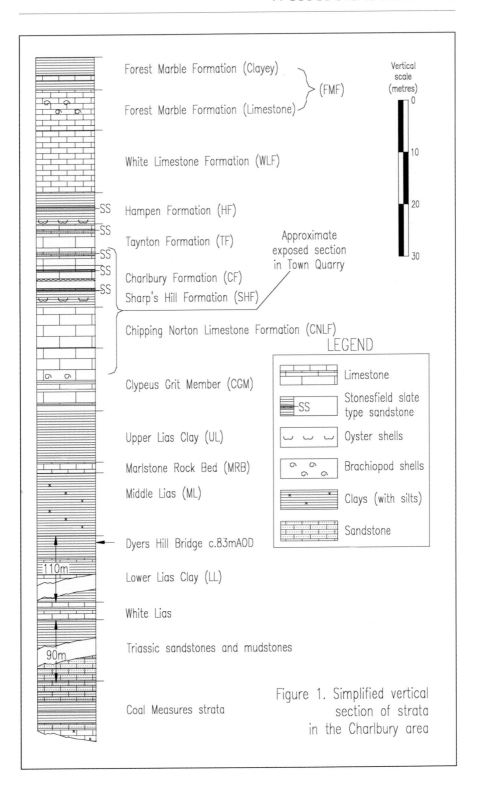

Forest Marble Formation (Clayey)
Forest Marble Formation (Limestone)
} (FMF)

Vertical
scale
(metres)

White Limestone Formation (WLF)

SS — Hampen Formation (HF)
SS — Taynton Formation (TF)

Approximate
exposed section
in Town Quarry

SS
SS — Charlbury Formation (CF)
SS — Sharp's Hill Formation (SHF)

Chipping Norton Limestone Formation (CNLF)

LEGEND

Clypeus Grit Member (CGM)

	Limestone
SS	Stonesfield slate type sandstone
	Oyster shells
	Brachiopod shells
	Clays (with silts)
	Sandstone

Upper Lias Clay (UL)

Marlstone Rock Bed (MRB)

Middle Lias (ML)

Dyers Hill Bridge c.83mAOD

110m

Lower Lias Clay (LL)

White Lias

Triassic sandstones and mudstones

90m

Coal Measures strata

Figure 1. Simplified vertical
section of strata
in the Charlbury area

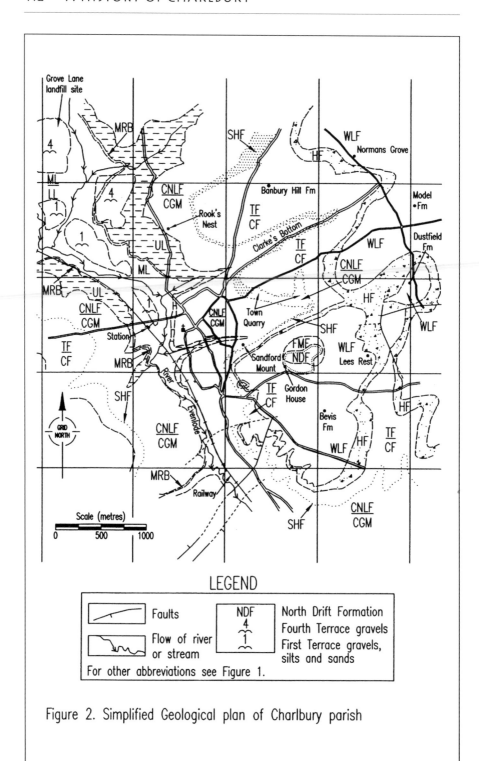

Figure 2. Simplified Geological plan of Charlbury parish

Way. It was formed in shallow water and has rootlets and plant remains; it may be a brackish water deposit in places and not entirely marine.

Locally the Hampen Formation is squeezed out by the **White Limestone** above. This limestone is about 10-15m thick and has an extensive outcrop on the more plateaux-like divides between valleys. It makes up the surface rocks at Dustfield Farm, Lee's Rest and Bevis Farm just beyond the parish boundary. The limestones are close grained, often porcellaneous and give a characteristic pale cream to white brash in the fields. A small quarry was worked for lime burning south-east of the Woodstock Road near the junction with Woody Lane and other small quarries were similarly worked for this limestone south of Woody Lane near Sandford Mount. The former cement works at Shipton on Cherwell used this limestone as a principal raw material.

The final bedrock strata at the top of the sequence within the parish boundary is the **Forest Marble Formation**. This occurs as an isolated outcrop of limestone around Gordon House, but is known only from field debris. It has been worked in the past from shallow pits in Wychwood and at Shipton Quarry and used for ornamental purposes since it is quite shelly and polishes well. The Forest Marble Formation is marked by intercalations of clay which dominate the upper part of the sequence of 7 to 9m. The clays are again quite sticky and where seen in trial pits at Gordon House were softened and much disturbed by periglacial effects.

A generalised geological section is given in Fig 1. A composite geological plan of the parish of Charlbury based on mapping by W J Arkell and the BGS is shown in Fig 2. Arkell's mapping in the 1940s is considered to be sound in the Charlbury area, especially his mapping of the Hampen Formation which was not consistently identified in the more rapid BGS mapping in the 1970s.

3 · SUPERFICIAL GEOLOGY

No further younger bedrock deposits occur inside the parish boundary although such strata of Jurassic age occur south and east of the Town. The Kellaways Clay and the Oxford Clay outcrop around Leafield and Combe. All subsequent strata which may have been formed have been eroded so that only materials which have been deposited much more recently in geological time occur near Charlbury. These are largely unconsolidated gravels, sands, silts and clays that date from the last 2 million years of the late Pliocene and Quaternary when glacial and warm interglacial periods occurred. They are present as thin debris draped over the local hills and valleys.

Classically in river valleys like that of the River Evenlode, there may be a series of terraces or incisions in the valley sides which denote previous stand positions of a river as it cuts its way through the bedrock. Often sands and gravels have been deposited on these terraces; the highest distinct river terraces are the oldest, and the lowest most recent. There are two well marked terraces with gravel within the parish boundary. The higher one, known by the BGS as the Fourth Terrace, remains largely intact, but was worked in small patches about 150 and 600m south-east of Coldron Mill. This terrace deposit is related to that just beyond the parish boundary on either side of Grove Lane, Spelsbury, which was extensively worked in the 1960s and 1970s. The gravels comprise poorly layered and much disturbed subrounded oolitic Jurassic limestone and also rounded quartzite pebbles. In the Grove Lane workings (which are now landfilled on the east and restored to woodland and ponds in the west) the gravels were generally 4-5m thick; they are thinner to the east inside the parish boundary. Observations by the BGS have led to the inference that this gravel was extensively disturbed by permafrost (or periglacial) conditions similar to those seen today in north Russia or Canada with features consistent with ice wedges and frost boils. The Fourth Terrace has been correlated with that at Long Hanborough and can be traced from the River Evenlode down the River Thames at least as far as to Maidenhead and Slough.

The Second and Third Terraces are not present around Charlbury but the First Terrace is present in the vicinity of the cricket ground. It is primarily a loamy silt with only occasional patches of gravel. In consequence there have been no recent attempts to work this deposit although a few hollows are still visible in the copse two fields east of Coldron Brook adjacent to the northern part of the Oxfordshire Way. This terrace, like the Fourth Terrace, can be correlated with other terraces along the River Evenlode and beyond to Oxford (the Northmoor Terrace).

The most enigmatic of the unconsolidated deposits are the quartz and quartzite gravels much rounded and almost certainly of Triassic (Bunter) age. These older gravels occur in places with sands, but are often embedded in clays and up to 2m thick. Generally the cobbles occur in the fields around the Town within the ploughed layer, mixed with stone brash.

This occurrence of foreign material in the Evenlode valley and high on the surrounding hills has excited academic interest for almost 200 years. For much longer, locals have gathered the larger cobbles from the fields and used them for forming paths and courtyards around houses in the centre of the Town. First reported by Buckland in 1820, he assumed the distribution of these gravels was due to the Biblical Flood.

Later this occurrence and distribution of Bunter cobbles was attributed to ice which was thought to have over-topped the Cotswold escarpment at Moreton-in-Marsh and travelled down the early, broad valley of the Evenlode and Thames as far as Reading. Certainly, when some excavations for building or settlement problems have been made such as those at Gordon House and in Lees Heights, the soft to firm brown silty clays containing the quartzite pebbles have a superficial appearance of a boulder clay or glacial till. This material was up to 3m thick in one location.

The most recent interpretation of these high level gravels is that they are water-lain and in places, where they are mixed with clay, this is probably due to later mixing with local clays during frozen ground conditions which existed during the Anglian Glaciation about 500,000 years ago. At least five different high level terraces have been identified by Rose and others which, when traced along the original path of the River Thames and the River Evenlode, overtop the lowest col of the Cotswold escarpment. It is over this escarpment, before it was eroded to its present state, that the Bunter pebbles came. Fragments of these terraces have been identified at Stag's Plain near Waterman's Lodge on the Cornbury Estate, on Ramsden Heath near the Nurseries and at Gordon House in Charlbury at ground levels ranging from 200m down to 150m. It is possible that some of these materials were laid down in an early River Evenlode/Thames which occupied a valley 8 to 10km wide running from north-west to south-east as far as Reading, before turning east and running along the Vale of St Albans into the sea in East Anglia north of the course of the present River Thames. Some of the material may have arrived at the early Cotswold escarpment at the time of the first, Cromerian, glaciation and represents wash-out deposits in the subsequent interglacial period. However, a number of workers in this area think that at some stage the River Evenlode/Thames extended upstream as far as the West Midlands and Wales on the basis of the range of pebbles found in this part of Oxfordshire.

At no time, certainly since the early Quaternary and possibly ever, has ice travelled down the Evenlode Valley as far as Charlbury. The nearest it reached, on the basis of significant glacial deposits is in the Moreton-in-Marsh area, between Broadwell and Kitebrook where it lies in the Evenlode Valley between 110 and 140m above sea level. Nevertheless, frozen ground conditions existed during the Middle Quaternary. The most obvious effects are demonstrated by the cambering and valley bulging features observed in the main Evenlode Valley as well as the side valleys. During frozen ground conditions water trapped in aquifers in valley bottoms expanded and heaved upwards, folding strata which would otherwise be sub-horizontal into an arch or anticlinal form often subsequently eroded when the ground thawed and rivers flowed again. On hillsides, strata cambered or slumped downwards over weakened materials such as clays, reducing the outcrop of the clays and giving rise to cracks or openings along joints in the overlying strata. These features are known as gulls and ridge and hollow features when greatly enlarged. They are parallel to valley sides and were first reported in the Charlbury area by Arkell in

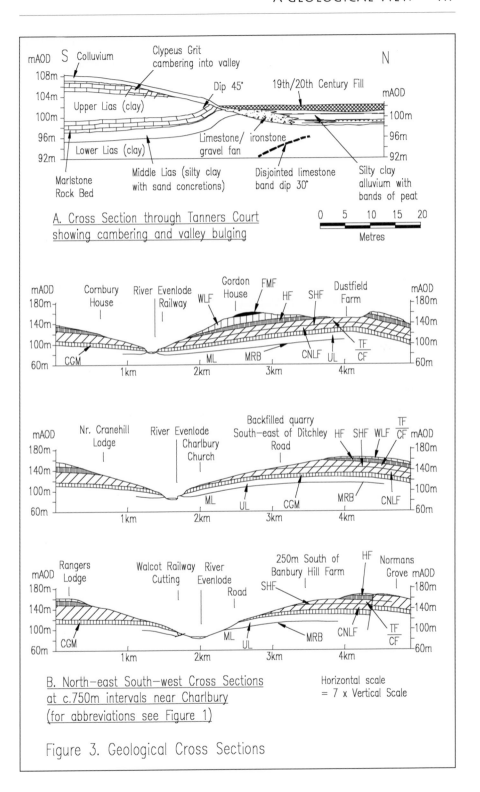

A. Cross Section through Tanners Court showing cambering and valley bulging

B. North-east South-west Cross Sections at c.750m intervals near Charlbury (for abbreviations see Figure 1)

Figure 3. Geological Cross Sections

1947. Cambering and valley bulging was obvious in the site investigation in Tanners Court referred to previously. Joint openings or gulls often extend a long way back from the centre line of the valley. Joint openings of more than 100mm were visible along faces in the Town Quarry during the 1980s consistent with movements towards Sandford Slade. The fields between the Oxfordshire Way near Bevis Farm and the Finstock/Fawler road show typical step-like, ridge and hollow features consistent with cambering movements, in this case several hundred metres from the River Evenlode.

From Dustfield Farm to its outcrop just below the junction of Dyer's Hill and Church Lane the base of the Jurassic limestones (Clypeus Grit) falls almost 30m in 2,500m. (See Fig 3). Not all this fall is thought to be due to cambering and valley bulging, a dome or antiform being centred near Dustfield Farm, but experience elsewhere suggests that as much as 50% may be due to cambering which could have developed over many tens of thousands of years of periglacial conditions around the time of the Anglian glaciation.

During frozen ground conditions the periods of summer thaw rendered the surface few metres more mobile. Clays with gravels could have slumped or slid down hill which may account for the distribution of some of the Bunter gravels over such a wide area. Frozen ground conditions are also represented by the fossil ice wedges and pipes previously seen in the Grove Lane gravel workings, in air photographs east of Charlbury and in small fossil ice polygons, seen in excavations at Stag's Plain and near Freeland.

4 · GEOLOGY AND THE DEVELOPMENT OF CHARLBURY

Groundwater and springs

As mentioned at the outset, the buildings in the Town in medieval and earlier times were concentrated just above the Clypeus Grit/Upper Lias Clay spring line. Wells in the centre of the Town are rarely more than 6m deep and were relatively easy to dig. Most of the older houses in the Town had a well, sometimes shared with neighbours, but it is quite common to find 2, 3 or even more wells having been dug near a single house and then back-filled with domestic rubbish. The clay bands in the Clypeus Grit commonly gave rise to permeability problems and caused silting-up. Often these wells are now inside properties which have extended at the rear of first building. Houses north-east of Market Street and Sheep Street (and away from the Sandford Slade stream) have an increasing depth to groundwater which may account for the reduced density of seventeenth and eighteenth century properties in this part of the Town. At the upper part of the Town along Ditchley Road and Hundley Way the depth to groundwater was often 10 to 12m or more, although well depths greater than this are known.

Piped water allowed a much easier development of the Town at the end of the nineteenth century and the spread of buildings is noticeable from this time. However, many properties still depended on wells into the 1930s and Sandford Mount even now maintains its own supply.

Groundwater flows down-dip beneath the Town so contaminants such as fuel oil at any point can lead to impacts on water quality at lower levels near to the River Evenlode. Such a situation may have occurred in 1928 with an alleged leak of arsenic from tanks in the leather tannery in Market Street. Wells in Church Lane were said to have been affected and the tannery was closed (to become initially a vehicle repair workshop). Similar considerations affected proposals by the then quarry operator in the 1970s to stop the use of the Town Quarry for landfilling since this could have polluted the aquifer with potential for leachates to occur in the Sandford Slade stream and ultimately the River Evenlode.

The same aquifer is still used by some houses and farms north of the Town even though most remaining wells in the Town were reported as condemned for drinking water in the 1950s. More outlying farms depended originally on supplies from the Charlbury Formation above the Sharp's Hill Formation Clays, e.g. Banbury Hill Farm or from the White Limestone above the Hampen Formation, e.g. Norman's Grove, Dustfield Farm and Lee's Rest. Much shallow groundwater around Charlbury and adjacent areas is now contaminated to a depth of 20-30m by high nitrate and nitrite levels from fertilisers used in agriculture and is not suitable for unrestricted use.

Little use has been made of the aquifer in the Marlstone Rock Bed probably because of its depth and difficult well sinking conditions. One bored well is known to have been specifically sunk to this level to supply water. The late Dr Humphrey Juler (*pers. com.*) found through one of his patients that, although water in this aquifer was potable, it had a high concentration of calcium sulphate (epsom salts) with disastrous consequences for visitors even though the locals were inured to the effects.

Foundations

With few exceptions, the Town has sound foundations where properties stand on limestones. There has been no history of large-scale instability due to geological features – rather problems have arisen locally due to building on or near rapidly changing ground conditions or clays especially in the side valleys such as Sandford Slade and in Lee's Heights where the Hampen Formation occurs. Other problems appear to be restricted to building over cellars or wells or backfilled quarries. There are no reported foundation difficulties associated with the Sharp's Hill Formation. However, there is some valley slope instability along the parish boundary at the former hamlet of Cote. Here the side stream to the Coldron Brook has cut down through the Upper Lias Clay and there are signs of slippage in the fields west of Coathouse Farm. The former settlement could have been affected by ground movements.

Charlbury Stone and other minerals

Reference has been made at various places to the use of the Chipping Norton Limestone in buildings in Charlbury. It is at first sight surprising that quarries were not located nearer to the Town since the same strata are accessible much closer to the Town centre. The reasons for the preponderance of quarry development off Ditchley Road and Hundley Way are uncertain; only one small quarry is shown near the Town centre on the 1870 OS plan; it lies just west of Mount Pleasant. However, it is known that across the Cotswolds the best stone, less affected by weathering and easier to dress, comes from beneath clays. It may therefore be no coincidence that most of the Town's many small quarries were developed north of the Slade where the Sharp's Hill Formation covered the Chipping Norton Limestone. A good impression of the extent of quarrying in and around the Town can be obtained from examining the details of the 1859 Tithe Remission Plan and accompanying key together with the 1st Edition Ordnance Survey 1:2500 plan of the area (1870). Some of these small quarries have subsequently been backfilled and built over in the 1960s. The main Town Quarry only seriously expanded from the 1960s to the 1990s when it produced fill materials for construction mostly out of Charlbury and sometimes out of the county. Latterly very little stone was worked for building.

Arkell described the use of Charlbury stone (Chipping Norton Limestone) in his book on Oxford Stone. The last Charlbury buildings constructed with new, local stone were the council houses along the Enstone Road, built about 1920. Charlbury stone was also used for Cowley Barracks before then. The same stone was previously worked in the nineteenth century near the old Saw Mill in Cornbury Park (Buckleap) and was found there, as in Charlbury, to weather well. The problem in Cornbury was that large blocks could not be obtained. Large blocks, some in excess of 5m^3, were present in the Town Quarry during the 1980s and 1990s but never used for dimension or walling stone for which they would have been well suited and have commanded a good price.

It is interesting to note that most of the older stone buildings in Charlbury were constructed using randomly coursed rubble walling, sometimes dressed, but with little use of dimension stone. The Town has relatively few buildings with ashlar facings except as strings or around windows; they seldom show detailed stonework at window and doorway openings compared with those in Chipping Norton or Burford. Victorian tour guides are known to refer to the poor, humble appearance of buildings in the Town. This certainly was not a function of the adequacy of the local raw material, but more probably a reflection of Charlbury's social or economic history.

It could be asked why Stonesfield Slate was not worked in Charlbury. The probable reason is that it is only in the latest workings of the quarry that slatey tilestones have been identified. There was probably no incentive to excavate quarries even further out of the Town. The only record of slate working inside the parish boundary is that of the 1859 tithe plan which notes 'slate pits' about 450m west of Ditchley Lodge to the south of the road (in the Hampen Formation). The slates were chiefly worked both beneath and around the valley-sides at Stonesfield. There may have been a number of exploratory shafts west of Stonesfield, one being near the junction of the Oxfordshire Way to Stonesfield and the track leading up to it from Fawler. Another may have been the shaft which opened up in Lee's Rest Farm about 450m south-west of the farmhouse a few years ago.

Other minerals have been worked fitfully around the Town; gravels have been worked locally towards Spelsbury as mentioned previously and ironstone was extracted at Fawler. Clays extracted at Fawler and Leafield were used for brick and pipe making as well as for pots but no attempt was made to extract clays for that purpose in the parish. Hearsay evidence suggests that small quantities of clay were excavated near the Spelsbury Road in Clarke's Bottom for use in colouring leather, allegedly in Somerset rather than in Charlbury, but there is little documentary evidence to confirm this. The tithe plan of 1859 does, however, refer to clay pits on the western rather than the eastern side of Pound Hill near Clarke's Bottom.

White Limestone was extracted in the nineteenth century from at least four small quarries near the Slade and Woodstock Road for lime burning in two kilns. Only the quarry along the Woodstock Road remains as evidence of this former widespread activity.

Geology today

As implied in the introduction, geology scarcely has an impact on modern-day life in Charlbury. Radon gas levels are somewhat raised in the lower parts of the Town and new buildings thereabouts are required to have adequate foundation ventilation to avoid accumulation of this harmful gas. Landfilling within and near Charlbury has now finished – the last site was at Dean Grove in Spelsbury, but it is less than a century since 'night soil' pails were removed from privies and spread over fields north east of the Town. Most shallow groundwater is now contaminated to some degree by intensive farming, but the Environment Agency will require careful investigations to be undertaken for a range of normal 'polluting' activities if they were to take place here. Activities such as fuel stations, cemetery extensions, agricultural waste disposal and even community compost heaps can excite this bureaucratic organisation. Any future building development, which many 'white settlers' want to avoid, will have to pay increasing attention to foundations, but no great difficulties beyond those noted above are likely to arise.

The Town Quarry remains a matter of interest. The existing quarry face near to Ditchley Road comprises a geological Site of Special Scientific Interest (SSSI) that now comes under the remote stewardship of English Nature. Some would like to see the whole site converted into a nature conservation area; developers for housing are also thought to be interested, and others in the Town consider the site suitable – given appropriate access – for a light industrial or commercial estate which the Town lacks. It is not yet a focus for fly tipping. The quarry was worked in later years with about 35% of the excavated material going back into the void as waste – chiefly the fines from crushing and screening and the Sharp's Hill and Charlbury Formation clays. This backfill, banked against the former quarry faces, was uncompacted and would require complete excavation and controlled compaction if the site were ever to be used for low-level built development. In addition, although the site is above the confined water table on the Upper Lias Clay, it forms a catchment of at least 10 hectares and receives groundwater from seepages above the Sharp's Hill Formation. Some ponding may eventually occur due to natural siltation and any significant development would require pumped surface water and sewage services. A proposal to extend the quarry to the east into Ditchley Estate land was made in 1989 and given planning permission; but the quarry operator omitted to obtain a binding agreement with the Estate! Scope still exists, if the Estate were so minded, to re-open quarrying, possibly with a revised access. Given the forthcoming imposition of the Aggregates Levy, the interest would probably be limited regarding low grade fill production. A more interesting development, unaffected by the levy, would be for the quarry to operate primarily (as in the more distant past) for the recovery of dimension and walling stone and possibly roofing tiles. Much slower rates of quarrying would be needed – probably less than a tenth of that previously. Stone processing could take place on site and provide opportunities which most of the previous proposals neglect.

Oddly, most geological activity in Charlbury is now, and for some time has been, of a professional nature. Following on from a successful quarry consultancy in Charlbury in the 1920s and 1930s run by Alfred Searle from offices at the top of Dyer's Hill, the author's firm employs about 25 geologists and engineers in quarrying work worldwide. Another smaller firm, Stewart Design in Park Street, works on specifying cladding dimension stone for buildings in Europe and America. Hence, although quarrying has ceased in the Town, related activities continue here for the benefit of a wider world than William Smith could have imagined 185 years ago when he first mapped the ground near Charlbury.

As to the future, it may be many millennia before real climate changes occur to radically alter earth surface processes such as erosion or deposition of sediments. Such changes are unlikely to be more dramatic than those which have happened in the geological past. Here in Charlbury the turbid melt waters of the snowfields on the Cotswolds produced gravels and cobbles for mammoths and bison to wander over. Earlier still the banks of shells and beaches by warm tropical seas were crossed by early vertebrates such as *Megalosaurus*. History is different when seen from a geological standpoint.

References

The most useful publications on the geology of Charlbury are by the British Geological Survey, especially *'Geological notes and local details for 1:10,000 sheet SP31NE Charlbury and Stonesfield'* by R J Wyatt (1981) and *'Geology of the Country around Chipping Norton'* by A Horton *et al* (1987). The equivalent report on *'Geology of the Country around Witney'* is nearly 60 years old and interpretations are significantly changed in many respects but the recently published *'Geology of the Cirencester District'* by Sumbler *et al* (2000) is quite helpful. During the 1970s local 1:10,000 geological plans for SP31 NW and NE and SP32 SW and SE were published and may be purchased from the BGS for £300 (£75 each). 2 1:50,000 geological plans Sheet Nos, 218 and 236 cover the area and are more modestly priced at £9 each.

Arkell's work in the *'Geology of Oxford'*, Clarendon Press (1947), is also dated but quite useful. His 1947 paper on the *'Geology of the Evenlode Gorge'* in the Proceedings of the Geologist's Association (PGA) for 1947 is very helpful. More recent papers of interest on bedrock matters, also published in the PGA are A J M Barron *et al 'A Revised Lithostratigraphy for the Inferior Oolite Group (Middle Jurassic) of the Cotswolds, England,' (1997)* B F W Boneham and R J Wyatt *'The Stratigraphical Position of the Middle Jurassic (Bathonian) Stonesfield Slate of Stonesfield, Oxfordshire'*, UK (1993) and R J Wyatt *'A correlation of the Bathonian (Middle Jurassic) succession between Bath and Burford, and its relation to that near Oxford'* (1996) and discussion in 1999. Also in the PGA, and dealing with superficial deposits, the following papers are useful: R W Hey *'A re-examination of the Northern Drift of Oxfordshire'* (1986); J Rose *et al 'The Kesgrave Sands and Gravels: 'pre-glacial' Quaternary deposits of the River Thames in East Anglia and the Thames Valley'* (1999) and M G Sumbler *'The Moreton Drift: A further clue to glacial chronology in Central England'* (2001).

The Coal Measures in Oxfordshire are described in outline by K C Dunham and E G Poole in *'The Oxfordshire Coalfield'* in the Journal of the Geological Society of London (1974) and *'A Correlation of Quaternary Deposits of the British Isles'* is given in Geological Society Special Report 23

(1999). An account of Fawler Ironstone mine is given in E S Tonk's *'The Ironstone Railways and Tramways of the Midlands'* (1959). Each of these papers or books includes other references the reader may find helpful to interpret the local geology.

Arkell also wrote *'Oxford Stone'* in 1947 which is a simple guide to local stones and the County Museum Services have produced useful publications on Stonesfield Slate and brick, tile and pottery manufacture in the county.

Finally, reference has been made to Practice files of various local projects and thanks is given to those knowingly or otherwise who have assisted. Special thanks must, however, be given to Dr Alan Cobb, one of the Practice partners, who has visited many of the local sites and assisted with amendments. The Partners have much appreciated the assistance and tolerance of the people of the Town during the 25 years that the firm has been in Charlbury.

Index

Other books from the Wychwood Press

Already in print:

Wychwood Forest and Its Border Places, John Kibble, 128pp £7.50

Charming Charlbury, Its Nine Hamlets and Chipping Norton, John Kibble, 224pp £10

Wychwood: The evolution of a wooded landscape, Beryl Schumer, 128pp £7.50

The Salt of the Earth: Diary of a poor family in Woodstock, 1900, Dorothy Calcutt, 128pp £7.50

'Walk Humble My Son': Growing Up in Ascott-Under-Wychwood, 1918-1939, Eric R. Moss, 144pp £8

The Forest that Sailed Away. Poems by Elizabeth Birchall, illustrations by Amanda Henriques, 64pp, £7.99

Discovering Wychwood: An Illustrated History and Guide, edited by Charles Keighley, 168pp £8.99

These books can be ordered from our office, post free in the UK. For details of new and forthcoming titles, please join our mailing list. Write to the address below, or (preferably) send your e-mail address to <carpenter@oxfree.com> and we'll notify you of new books by e-mail.

You are also welcome to visit our bookshop, Evenlode Books, at our Charlbury address, where we keep a wide range of books of local interest.

The Wychwood Press
Alder House, Market Street, Charlbury OX7 3PH
Tel / fax   01608 811969